Catch Rope

The Long Arm of the Cowboy

The History and Evolution of Ranch Roping

Number One: Western Life Series

Cover photo: John A. Stryker photograph courtesy of Texas and Southwestern Cattle Raisers Foundation, Fort Worth, Texas.

Catch Rope

The Long Arm of the Cowboy

by

John R. Erickson

University of North Texas Press

10 9 8 7 6 5 4 3 2 1

Permissions
University of North Texas Press
Post Office Box 13856
Denton, Texas 76203-6856

Library of Congress Cataloging-in-Publication Data

Erickson, John R., 1943–
Catch rope : the long arm of the cowboy : the history and evolu-
tion of ranch roping / by John R. Erickson.
        p.   cm.   — (Western life series ; 1)
Includes index.
ISBN 0-929398-66-1
1. Calf roping—History. 2. Lasso. I. Title. II. series.
GV1834.45.C34E75   1994
791.8'4—dc20   93–35820
                                                                CIP

The paper used in this book meets the minimum requirements of the
American National Standard for Permanence of Paper for Printed Library
Materials, Z39.48.1984. Binding materials have been chosen for durability.

Cover photo: John A. Stryker photograph courtesy of Texas and Southwestern Cattle Raisers Foundation, Fort Worth, Texas.

Cover design by Aaron Pendland

"Swinging a rope is all right if your neck ain't in it."
—Will Rogers

"Ropes, like guns, are dangerous. All the difference is, guns go off and ropes go on."
—Charlie Russell

"Let any man, beast, or idea present a daring target to a cowboy, and he will spread his loop with strangulation and fun on his mind."
—J. P. S. Brown

Contents

Part Two: Roping Stories

Preface

The old-time cowboy was a workingman. He was shaped and defined by his work. Like most of us, he was at his best when he was doing his job, using his tools and skills to accomplish difficult tasks. He used many tools in his work, but the two that have become most closely identified with him are the horse and the catch rope. The skilled use of these two pieces of equipment was essential if a man wanted to follow the horseback life.

The horse was the cowboy's means of transportation. It took him where he wanted to go, regardless of the weather or the terrain. Once he got there, the rope was the tool he used to extend his reach and subdue animals that were much larger and stronger than he. It was the "long arm of the cowboy."

Writers and scholars have devoted a good deal of attention to the western horse, and as a result we have an accurate record of the early cowhorses: what they looked like (they were smaller than the horses of today and, by modern standards, not so pretty); how they performed (they were tough little brutes); and how the early mustang-bred cowhorse evolved, through careful breeding, into the animals we use today.

The cowboy's other tool, the catch rope, has not received nearly as much attention. Several good books have been written on the *charro* and *vaquero* traditions of roping which originated in Mexico, and in recent years a number of good studies about arena roping have appeared, written by rodeo cowboys like Leo Camarillo who have found a way to make a living by throwing a rope. But these studies cover the two ends of the spectrum, leaving a big gap in the center. Occupying that space is the American ranch cowboy who, for the past century, has used his rope as an everyday tool. The cowboy has drawn from both ends of the tradition but is neither a *charro* nor a PRCA champion. Hence, as David Dary pointed out in *Cowboy Culture*, "The definitive book on stock roping has yet to be written" (p. 351).

Between 1974 and 1981 I worked as a full-time ranch cowboy in the Texas and Oklahoma Panhandles. During that time the catch rope was one of the tools of my trade. I used it almost every day. I worked hard to become proficient at roping, and took pride in my skill. By the time I retired from active cowboying, I had become as good a roper as I needed to be. Out in the pasture, I was able to use the rope to take care of the jobs that needed to be done. I'm not interested in trying to convince anyone that I was a great roper, because I wasn't. I could list a dozen men I rode with who were better hands with the rope than I. But knowing how much you don't know is in itself a valuable piece of knowledge.

The qualification I bring to this study of ranch roping is that I devoted eight years to studying the craft of roping in its natural medium, the pasture. At the same time, I was pestering old-time cowboys with questions about roping, and reading everything I could find that had been written on the subject. I've been working on this project for fifteen years now. I've gathered roping stories in some strange places: ahorseback in Texas, Oklahoma, and New Mexico; around dinner tables; in cow lots and back yards and bookstores. You never know when or where you're liable to run into somebody who can tell you something new about roping. Why would anybody want to collect roping stories? I don't know, except that I've always admired good ropers, always wanted to be pretty good at it myself, and never wanted the knowledge of the old-time ropers to slip behind the veil of time.

Sometime around 1978 I noticed that nobody had ever done a study on the history and evolution of pasture roping, and although I could think of several men who were better qualified than I to do such a study, I knew they wouldn't because they were full-time cowboys. So I decided to do it. The purpose of this book is to fill in some of the gaps in our knowledge of ranch roping: where it came from, how it evolved, how the rope was used by the old-timers, and how it is used by cowboys on modern day ranches.

Notice that I said *ranch roping*. There's a big difference between ranch roping and the kind of roping that's done in the rodeo arena. There are points of similarity, since arena roping has been a major influence on the techniques used by today's cowboys. But there are important differences between the two. What works in the pasture rarely works in the arena, and what works in the arena sometimes fails in the pasture.

In other words, this isn't a training manual for young fellows who want to go to the arena and win some money. Books of that nature are around, and they've been written by professional ropers who've made a thorough study of competition roping. The techniques I'll be describing all derive from pasture work, and if a guy starts playing around with these throws, it's liable to mess him up when he goes back to speed roping in the arena.

When possible, I've drawn on historical sources, but these sources are few and sketchy, so as we go along, I'll rely more and more on my own observations of cowboying in Texas and Oklahoma. If I can't present a perfect reconstruction of pasture roping in the past, at least I can make an accurate record of present methods for future generations.

The last chapter of this book is what scholars refer to as a "critical bibliography," a list of books, articles, interviews, and correspondence I referred to in my research, along with my comments about them. Just as I don't try to palm myself off as a great roper, I don't consider myself a great scholar. There may be dozens of important sources I've missed, among them all the books that have been written by rodeo cowboys who rope in competition. I didn't list those sources because I don't refer to them in the text.

Incidentally, several chapters in this book appeared in different form in *The Cattleman, Western Horseman,* and *Livestock Weekly.*

Before we go on, I ought to pass out roses to my teachers, the old boys out on the ranches who took the time to share their knowledge with me: Stanley Barby, Jake Parker, Glenn Green, Pat Mason,

Joe Stiles, Bob Walker, Tom Ellzey, Lawrence Ellzey, Bill Ellzey, Jim Streeter, Buster Welch, Dave Nicholson, Bud Reed, Floyd Koch, Frankie McWhorter, Dan Cockrell, Chet Norman, Curt Brummett, Greg Hale, Frank Bridwell, and Sam Sherman. Thanks also to the scholars who steered me toward written sources: David Dary, Paul Patterson, Marc Simmons, and Dr. J. S. Palen.

I am grateful to the following people and organizations for allowing me to use their illustrations in this book: Madge Reid of Ace Reid Enterprises, Kerrville, Texas; Sonja Clayton, Abilene, Texas; Kris Erickson, Perryton, Texas; the Texas and Southwest Cattle Raisers Foundation in Fort Worth; and the Amon Carter Museum, Fort Worth, Texas.

I want to thank Fran Vick, Charlotte Wright, and the other folks at the University of North Texas Press for publishing this book and working with me to improve it.

And finally, thanks to my wife, Kris Erickson, who has been a great partner through twenty-six years of work and marriage.

Part One

History and Technique

1

Who Were the First Ropers?

When today's cowboy goes out into the pasture and dabs his twine in something, he doesn't stop to wonder how he came to have a rope in his hands—who invented it or where his technique originated. If you asked him where he learned to rope, he might tell you that he learned from Larry Joe over on the next ranch, and that Larry Joe picked it up from Charlie, who used to go to town on Sundays and rope in the arena. And there the questioning would probably hit a stone wall. But there's one thing we can be sure of: although the modern cowboy has added a new twist here and there, the basic technology of roping has been around for a long time.

Our great-grandfathers, at least those who were cowboys, knew how to rope. They carried grass instead of nylon on their horn string. They probably tied hard-and-fast to the horn, and they made throws we don't hear much about these days—the Blocker, the hoolihan, the back-handed slip catch, and other throws that no one ever bothered to name. But *they* didn't invent roping either. They learned from someone else.

It's common knowledge that our great-grandfathers picked up roping from Mexican vaqueros, skilled in the use of the rawhide reata centuries before Texas became the cradle of the cattle industry. In *Cowboy Culture*, David Dary notes that by the seventeenth century the vaqueros of New Spain (Mexico) had learned to make excellent use of their reatas and that their techniques had improved through the years.

Dary does not attempt to trace roping beyond Mexico, nor does he ask where or how the vaqueros discovered it. But he does point out that before 1573, the cowboys of New Spain used a device called the *luna*, or hocking knife, a long pole armed with a sharpened steel blade on one end. Mounted on a running horse, the rider manipulated his lance and used it to hamstring a wild cow, which was then dispatched and skinned for its hide. These horsemen in colonial Mexico were so proficient in the use of the hocking knife that herds of cattle were decimated, and in 1574 the hamstringing of cattle was outlawed. Anyone caught carrying a lance was required to pay a fine of twenty pesos or receive a hundred lashes in public. It was then, Dary believes, that roping appeared in Mexico, replacing the hocking knife as a pasture tool.

"Contrary to the belief of some," Dary observes, "most sixteenth-century vaqueros did not circle their rope in the air above them and throw the loop over the horns of cows. That technique was developed later. In the sixteenth century a vaquero put the loop on the end of his lance and then, from atop his horse, raced after a cow"(p. 21). He eased the loop over the animal's horns and took out the slack. What did he do with the home-end of the rope? "The other end of the rope was either tied to the cinch on the vaquero's saddle or to his horse's tail," Dary explains (p. 21). I expect that any modern cowboy who has ever gotten a hot rope in the vicinity of his pony's tail-section would want to see this technique demonstrated several times before he tried it himself.

Spur Ranch, Texas, 1909. A Spur cowpuncher making a good catch in the remuda as the horses attempt to dodge his lariat. *Ervin E. Smith photograph, 1909. Courtesy of The Ervin E. Smith Collection of the Library of Congress on deposit at the Amon Carter Museum, Fort Worth, Texas. Museum Number LC S6–285.*

We know on good authority that vaqueros in New Spain were using the rope by the year 1574. We also know that some Plains Indians practiced an elementary form of roping. In *The Comanches*, Ernest Wallace and E. Adamson Hoebel report that "lassoing was a popular Comanche method of capturing wild horses, even though relatively few animals were taken in this manner. It was an art in which the Comanche was often an expert" (p. 42). Victor Tixier, a Frenchman who spent several months with the Osage Indians in 1840, saw these northern Indians capture wild horses with a lariat held on the end of a forked stick. In 1805 Lewis and Clark noted that the Shoshones, Nez Perce, and Flatheads were expert at roping running horses. But none of these accounts is very helpful since they don't provide the reader with details that might explain where the Indians learned to rope or how long they had known about it. These references are typical of most of what has been written about old-time roping: short on details, long on questions.

We might surmise that the Comanches picked up a few roping skills through their contact with the Mexican vaqueros. Josiah Gregg, who explored the southwestern prairies in the years 1840–47, observed vaqueros using their ropes, "usually made of horse-hair, or sea-grass tightly twisted together," to catch wild horses. Gregg claimed that after roping a horse by the neck, the vaquero would often "throw a *bozal* (or half-hitch, as boatmen would say) around the nose, though at full rope's length." Gregg also noted that the Mexicans sometimes used their ropes as weapons. "In skirmishes with the Indians, the mounted vaquero, if haplessly without arms, will throw this formidable object round the neck or the body of his enemy, who, before he has time to disencumber himself, is jerked to the ground and dragged away at full speed" (pp. 131–32).

That might explain how the Comanches discovered roping. But what about the Osages, Shoshones, Flatheads, and Nez Perces? Could the techniques of the vaquero have been transmitted that far north of the Rio Grande? Did the early French explorers come to the New World with a knowledge of roping? Or had the Indians discovered the rope on their own and used it for centuries before the Spaniards and the French arrived? We don't know, and there is probably no way of finding out. So the questions remain: What were the antecedents of roping in the New World? Did the European explorers invent roping, or had it been introduced to them in the Old World before they came to the Americas?

In a fascinating little book called *Dark and Dashing Horsemen*, the late Stan Steiner suggested that the rope was used by the ancient Persians:

> Of all the innovations of the Persians, none had a more startling effect on horsemanship than did the lassos they perfected. Perhaps they learned the use of the thrown lasso from the herdsmen of their mountain tribes, for such lassos had been used by nomadic shepherds in many regions of the world long before the Persians developed them into weapons. (pp. 37–38)

Steiner goes on to say that, at a time when the lariat was unknown to Europeans, the Mongol warriors of Genghis Khan picked up roping techniques from the Persians and in battle used the rope with uncanny accuracy, catching an enemy "as though he were a half-wild Asian cow. It was a fighting method that was to have a shocking effect upon the dignity of the knights of Europe" (p. 55).

It is unfortunate that Steiner didn't document the sources of this information, but if he is correct, then the technology of roping is much older than most of us have supposed, and the Mexican vaquero stands in the middle, not at the beginning, of a very long evolutionary line which began three or four thousand years ago with mountain herdsmen in Persia, was passed on to the Persian and Mongol warriors who used it as a weapon of war, and then to the Berbers, Moors, and Arabs who invaded Spain in the seventh century A.D.

Is that as far back as we can take roping? Dary has responded to that question.

> Rope *appears* to have been among man's earliest tools, probably older than written history. Bill Severn in his

book *Rope Roundup* . . . observes that braided rope of animal hide was made in southwest Asia before 4000 B.C., because "some of the pottery of that period has patterns that were formed by pressing spun cord into the clay." Unfortunately, Severn does not cite his specific sources. (Letter to the author, February 1982).

It comes as a shock to most of us cowboys to learn that ropes have been around for 6000 years, yet there's reason to believe that people may have been using them even earlier. In a book called *Atlantis: The Eighth Continent,* Charles Berlitz quotes the Greek philosopher Plato on the subject of the lost civilization of Atlantis:

> There were bulls who had the range of the temple of Poseidon; and the ten who were left alone in the temple, after they had offered prayers to the gods that they might take the sacrifices that were acceptable to them, hunted the bulls without weapons, but with staves and nooses; and the bull which they caught they led up to the column. (pp. 48–49)

If the Atlanteans were hunting bulls with *nooses,* they were using catch ropes, which means that the origins of this cowboy tool might be traced back 12,000 to 20,000 years into the mists of human memory.

Beyond that, we needn't go. But we can be sure that we didn't invent the rope. Neither did our great-grandfathers, and neither did the Mexican vaqueros from whom they learned. We're all using a tool that has been around for a long, long time, and the fact that it is still in use today is a pretty good indication that it's a handy piece of equipment.

2

Out of Mexico: Vaqueros and Cowboys

We don't know much about the first ropers, the Atlanteans, Persians, Mongols, Moors, and Spaniards of the Old World, but we have a fairly accurate record of roping once it got into the hands of Mexican vaqueros and moved northward into the United States. To understand what happened to roping once it crossed the border, we must look at the two different traditions that developed more than a century ago and are still in place today: the vaquero tradition and the cowboy tradition. No one has given a better explanation of the historical roots behind these two traditions than Arnold Rojas, an old California vaquero who had the vision of a true scholar in spite of the fact that he only completed the third grade in school. In a book called *Vaqueros and Buckeroos*, Rojas writes:

> Although the terms "cowboy," "vaquero," and "buckaroo" have in the past been used interchangeably and indiscriminately, to do so is not accurate . . . because there is a vast difference between them. . . . In the United States there are two systems or styles of working cattle, or, rather, two kinds of herdsmen. One, the vaquero, is Hispanic in origin; the other, the cowboy, is African in origin. . . . The vaquero or buckaroo is a Westerner in fact. The cowboy is a Southerner. . . .
>
> The cowboy's territory is east of the Rockies; the vaquero's is west of this great barrier. The vaquero or buckaroo is unlike the cowboy in many ways: [his] racial background, lingo, character, methods of working cattle, and conception of what a horseman should be are different. (pp. 117)

We can only guess where Mr. Rojas came up with his "African" hypothesis, since he doesn't list any sources for his opinions. His point, I gather, is that cattle work in the Old South was done by blacks, who developed methods of horsemanship and roping to accomplish their work. These methods were then adopted by white herdsmen who carried them west into Texas and beyond, and established them as the cowboy (southern) tradition.

It's an interesting theory and there is probably some truth in it, although it ignores the obvious and well-documented influence of Northern Mexico on the equipment and methods of the cowboy. I think the distinction Rojas wanted to make between the two herding traditions was not Hispanic/African or western/southern, but rather aristocratic/plebian. Vaqueros, in his view, were special beings, descendants of European knights in armor, and keepers of a high code of conduct. Cowboys, on the other hand, came from the unwashed masses: poor whites, Southern blacks, and the péons of Northern Mexico. Although Rojas takes an eccentric and self-serving view of history, he is exactly right in concluding that two distinct methods of riding and roping appeared in the United States at approximately the same time: cowboy and vaquero/buckaroo.

American cowboys learned a great deal about roping from their counterparts in Mexico. This photo pictures Brahman cattle and Mexican ranch hands from the 1950s. *Courtesy of Texas and Southwestern Cattle Raisers Foundation, Fort Worth, Texas.*

He goes on to list the specific differences between the two groups. The first is in the area of horsemanship: "[The vaquero's] pride was in having a bridle hand; the cowboy had to have a horse that knew more about working cattle than its rider." The second is on the subject of bitting: "[The vaquero] is a palate-bit man. He uses a leather curb-strap [and] does not depend on leverage so much as on the signal of the port touching the palate." On the subject of saddles, Rojas says the vaquero used a "center-fire" or single-rigged saddle, meaning that it had only one cinch around the horse's belly, while the cowboy's saddle was double-rigged, with a front cinch and a roping cinch behind it. The cowboy maintained that the double-rigged saddle worked better in roping heavy animals, while the vaquero maintained that the single-rig was kinder to a horse's back.

Style versus speed was a major area of difference. The vaquero was more concerned with style than speed, while the cowboy placed those matters in reverse order, according to Rojas.

> The West Coast rider abhorred the plain equipment of the Gulf Coast rider; in it he found no silver, no beauty, no pride in possession or profession. . . . To the vaquero it was undignified to throw a rope hurriedly. . . . While pursuing his calling, [the vaquero] never forgot, wherever he found himself, that merit lay not only in what he did, but also in how he did it.

Ropes were another sign of difference. The cowboy carried a short (twenty-five to thirty-foot) rope of grass composition and tied it solid to the saddle horn, while the vaquero used a long (up to sixty feet and sometimes even longer) reata of plaited leather, and dallied (wrapped) the home-end around the horn (pp. 117–43).

To people not involved in the cattle business, these differences between vaqueros and cowboys might seem insignificant, but they are extremely important to a study of today's ranch roping, where it came from and how it developed.

By the 1880s each of the two schools of roping had established its territory. The cowboy tradition had taken root in the prairie states east of the Rockies, while the vaquero/buckeroo tradition held the country from the Rockies to the Pacific Ocean, and also in South Texas, according to new evidence offered by Joe S. Graham. Until fairly recent times, if a man came from California, Nevada, or Oregon you could assume that he was a long rope and dally man. If he came from Texas, Oklahoma, or Kansas, you could assume that he carried a short rope and tied to the horn.

Arnold Rojas writes, "We thus find the California rider distinct not only in costume, custom, speech and character, but also in nature, from the other riders or herdsmen of the New World, including those of central Mexico" (p.123). He defines the territory of the vaquero as "the part of North America lying west of the Rocky Mountains, and the part of Mexico lying west of the Sierra Madre, from the Tropic of Cancer to Canada" (p. 123).

Yet nothing is ever quite as simple as it ought to be. Indeed, I have encountered a puzzle in my own family background. My great-grandfather, Joe Sherman, was raised by cowboys on the Loving Ranch west of Fort Worth, and became a pioneer rancher in West Texas. This would have put him in the heart of the prairie cowboy tradition of roping. Yet Max Coleman, in his book *From Mustanger to Lawyer*, described Grandfather Sherman this way:

> He always carried what was called a California rope. That was a sixty-foot coil of hard manila rope on the right side of his saddle. He could also skillfully throw it, being one of the best men with a rope I ever saw. The usual rope carried in the '90s was only thirty-five feet. This long coil of rope was a style of rope which came from California. However, I never saw a longer coil of rope carried than that of Joe Sherman, when I worked on the Miller and Lux Ranch in Lower California, where the Mexican vaqueros prided themselves on their long coils of rope. (p. 140)

A sixty-foot rope in West Texas? When I read that, I was astounded. If he carried that big coil of rope, then he had to be a dally man—in a region where taking dallies was almost against the law! In September of 1993, I had occasion to ask my second cousin, Sam Sherman, about this. Sam, who cowboyed and ranched in New Mexico until recent years, said that it was true: Joe Sherman was a long-rope-and-dally man, and he passed that tradition on to his oldest son Forrest (Sam's father and my great-uncle).

> My father wouldn't have dreamed of letting us rope wild stock, tied hard-and-fast. It was too dangerous. When we got ourselves into a storm, he wanted us to give up our ropes. We always got them back. Sometimes a bull would carry a rope through that Pecos River country for several days, but eventually we got it back.

Sam also mentioned that Forrest Sherman dallied even when he was heeling calves in the herd at branding time, and that he might rope all day in the herd without missing a loop.

So where did Great-grandfather Sherman become a long-rope-and-dally cowboy? We know that he left home at the age of thirteen and took part in the great Traildriving Era recently depicted in the book and movie *Lonesome Dove,* and that he stayed in Nebraska and worked on a ranch for a year or more. There, perhaps, he worked with buckaroos from Montana or California who taught him their methods, which he then took back to West Texas—where, I would bet a good pair of boots, he was the only man who carried sixty feet of twine.

This incident, involving my own kinfolks, should serve as a reminder that nobody's theory about the evolution of roping is bullet-proof—not mine or Mr. Rojas's or anyone else's. It shows that the line between the cowboy and vaquero traditions was never impenetrable, and that even in the 1890s there was an exchange of ideas between them.

We know, for example, that there were states where the two traditions of roping existed side by side. Study Charlie Russell's paint-ings of Montana cowboys and you'll see that they all carried big coils of rope and none is tied hard-and-fast to the horn: *Roping A Wolf,*

Wild Horse Hunters, The Broken Rope, Tight Dally and Loose Latigo, A Moment of Great Peril, and *Loops and Swift Horses Are Surer Than Lead.*

After viewing Russell's work, you'd be inclined to think that everybody in Montana subscribed to the dally method, but old Spike Van Cleve spent his life ranching near Big Timber, Montana, and wrote some fine books about it, and he was a tie-solid, double-rigged, short rope cowboy to his dying day, and held dally ropers in magnificent contempt (Interview, 1978). Montana hosted both traditions of roping because it was settled from two directions—by Texas cowboys who went up the great cattle trails from the Gulf Coast and decided to stay in Montana, and by buckaroos from Oregon who brought in cattle from the West.

Arizona is another state with a dual tradition. According to the Rojas formula, Arizona should be a vaquero state, yet how do we account for this passage in *Hashknife Cowboy*, where the narrator is an Arizona cowboy named Mack Hughes?

> Then the men got to discussin' the merits of tie-hard-and-fast and dally roping. Some of them got into a heated argument. I didn't really know any dally-men myself, as Pat and every cowboy I knew in the Tonto Basin "took their dallies in the morning when they saddled up," meaning, of course, that they tied their ropes hard and fast and left 'em that way. (p. 28)

Once again Rojas finds the answer in history: "The cowboy got as far west as central Arizona. There the two systems—one Spanish, the other African—clashed. It was in the nature of things that when the West Coast rider met the Gulf Coast rider there would be friction" (p. 125). Some of the friction between practitioners of the two roping methods still exists today. It often focuses on the endless argument over which is the better method, dallying the rope or tying solid to the horn (which we will take up in a later chapter). But it goes deeper than that, into matters of personal style and taste.

I know a Texas cowboy who went to Nevada and worked on a

A Tight Dally and a Loose Latigo, by Charles M. Russell, 1920.
Courtesy of the Amon Carter Museum, Fort Worth, Texas. Museum number 1961.196.

buckaroo outfit for a while. He told me that he was never able to fit in there, that the buckaroos never accepted him and looked down on him as an outsider. Of course, he never accepted their ways either: "I saw guys going out and spending all their wages on silver bits and spurs, while their families were at home with nothing. That just didn't seem right to me." It wasn't long until he returned to Texas (Dave Nicholson, Interview, 1982).

If the buckaroos look down on the prairie cowboys because they lack style, the cowboys often perceive the buckaroos as vain and arrogant, just a little too preoccupied with their appearance and style. One certainly gets a whiff of that arrogance in the writings of Arnold Rojas. The man is a fine writer and an original thinker of high order, but his arguments always seem to funnel down to the conclusion that the vaquero is a superior being. For that reason, it is hard for a prairie cowboy to read his work without clenching his teeth at least part of the time.

But even though buckaroos and cowboys continue to clash over matters of style, much of the steam has gone out of the tie-hard-or-dally debate. Why? Because within the last twenty-five years the dally method has moved into the prairie states and has become the accepted method of doing business on many ranches. Since that is a change of major proportions, and since it occurred without a shot having been fired by either side, I'll devote the next chapter to sketching out how it happened.

3

Dally or Tie?

There's a moral to my story, boys,
And that you all must see.
Whenever you go to tie a snake
Don't tie it to your tree;
But take your dolly welters
'Cording to California law,
And you'll never see your old rim-fire
Go drifting down the draw.
—"Windy Bill," an old cowboy song

"Kill thy horse, kill thyself, but rope and hang on."
—Motto of South Texas brush cowboys

As we saw in the previous chapter, the dally method followed Hispanic cowboys out of Mexico and took root in California, Oregon, Nevada, and parts of Montana and Arizona. The cowboys who, in time, would establish the hard-tie tradition of roping migrated from the eastern and southern states and began settling in Texas in the 1820s.

When they arrived in Texas, these settlers, especially those from the north, were riding hornless saddles of English extraction, which would have made any type of roping difficult, if not impossible. "There were few saddlehorns of prominence," David Dary tells us in *Cowboy Culture*. "These eastern saddles were made for riding and not for working cattle" (p. 77). Once in Texas, settlers discovered the Spanish saddles that had been used by vaqueros in Mexico since the Conquest. These saddles had been changed from the original Conquistador design, which was a war saddle, into a device better suited for handling livestock. Among the changes Mexican horsemen made was adding a saddle horn. "The Texians soon adopted the vaquero's saddle, either trading for or buying them from vaqueros." Or they made their own, "with a large saddlehorn styled after the Mexican vaquero's" (p. 77). They also adopted his method of roping, but only for a short time.

As Fay Ward noted, "The early Texas cowhands were all reata-and-dally men until the hard-twist rope made its appearance" (p. 155). Then they began tying the home-end of their ropes to the horn. The record is not clear on exactly when this occurred, but it coincided with the aquisition by Texas cowboys of horned saddles AND with the appearance of a vegetable fiber rope that could stand the jerk of half a ton of meat without breaking.

Why did the Texas boys change from the dally to the hard-and-fast method? That question seems to have been overlooked by historians, even by the meticulous Professor Dary. Why would Texas cowboys who had learned most of their stock-handling techniques from the vaqueros NOT continue their method of roping? One writer who has addressed this question is Arnold Rojas, the California vaquero. In what may be the most insulting passage ever written about prairie cowboys, Rojas argued that they tied solid *because they rode such poor horses and were such inept horsemen that they couldn't have done otherwise*:

> He tied his rope, not because of a disregard for the consequences, but because he had to have two hands to guide his horse. He could never learn to take turns

This rope is tied hard and fast to the horn with a figure-eight knot. Some cowboys prefer to build their horn loop by plaiting the rope, using a rawhide "keeper" or even using a link of chain.

Courtesy of photographer, Kris Erickson.

The terms "dally," "dolly," and "dolly welters" were corruptions of the Span-ish *darale vuelta*, meaning "give it a turn." Here, the cowboy has dallied his rope on a horn wrapped with strips of inner tube, which holds the rope better than a slick leather horn. Some cowboys wrap their horns with cotton rope or mulehide. Dallies should be taken with the thumb pointing up. A thumb pointed the wrong way sometimes ends up on the ground. *Courtesy of photographer, Kris Erickson.*

around the horn to hold a beef. The truth of the matter is that the cowboy adopted the methods he used,
not from choice, but from the pressure of circumstances. (p. 125)

Mr. Rojas's book contains neither chapter notes nor a bibliography, so it is impossible to tell if this passage reflects only his opinions
or if he has drawn on historical sources. But there is probably *some*
truth in what he says. Certainly the people who settled Texas from
the eastern states were amateur horsemen, compared to the vaqueros
of California, and the horses couldn't have been much better than
their riders.

But I don't think poor horsemanship is the complete answer to
the question of why some Texas cowboys adopted a totally different
style of roping. I would guess that the impatience of the Anglo cowboys was at least as much a factor as their horsemanship. By tem-
perament, they were less inclined to give slack, either to livestock or
to humans, than their Hispanic counterparts. It may be an accident of
language that "dally" in English means "to play, trifle, or loiter," but
that probably describes the way those early Texas cowboys viewed
the vaquero method of capturing wild stock. My *Webster's New World
Dictionary* says that the English word "dally" derives from the Middle
English *dalien* and the Old French *dalier*, while the roping term "dally"
is a corruption of the Spanish term, *darle vuelta*, "give it a turn."
Hence, although it is tempting to speculate on the similarities between the English word and the cowboy's view of dally roping, there
is probably no basis for it. Still, to dally the rope, to give slack, to
wear the animal down, was, to the Anglo cowboy, to waste time.

Once they were equipped with stock saddles and hard-twist
ropes, the early Texas cowboys began gathering wild cattle out of the
South Texas brush country. One such cowboy was young Abel Head
"Shanghai" Pierce, who later became a wealthy cattle baron in South
Texas. In *Shanghai Pierce: A Fair Likeness*, Chris Emmett tells us that
as early as 1853, Shanghai was roping and branding wild cattle around
Matagorda Bay (p. 53). Unfortunately, Emmett tells us nothing about
the type of saddle he rode or how he handled his rope. Like many

accounts of old-time cowboys, Emmett's book does not have a single entry in the index for ropes or roping. Most likely Pierce rode a modified vaquero saddle, and tied his rope solid to the horn. Anyone familiar with the character of Shanghai Pierce would find it hard to believe that he had the patience to dally his rope, give slack, or follow the methods of the Hispanic horsemen.

I would imagine that in Shanghai Pierce, we find the typical qualities of the pre-Civil War Anglo cowboys who developed the hard-and-fast method of roping: he was young, brash, and in a hurry to make his fortune. After the Civil War, when the great trail herds began moving north towards the railheads in Kansas and Missouri, saddle design reflected the needs of hard-and-fast roping. On page 195 of *The Cowboy At Work*, Fay Ward has an illustration of an "old-style Texas iron-horn saddle . . . that was used by a majority of old-time trail drivers." The iron horn and back cinch identify it as the rig of a hard-and-fast roper. Hence, we can assume that by 1870, and perhaps even earlier, the hard-and-fast method had become standard in Texas and other areas that had not been touched by the dally tradition of the vaquero. Once in place, it became almost a rule of law, and so it remained until the middle of the present century. But by the 1950s the dally method was being exported to non-dally states by non-Hispanic cowboys who had learned it in the roping arena, where dallying was required in team roping. From the arena, it moved out onto the ranches.

When I was cowboying in the Texas and Oklahoma Panhandles near the end of the 1970s, *most* of the ranch cowboys I knew used the dally method. Some had started out roping in the hard-and-fast tradition and had made the switch to the dally. Others had come of age when everyone dallied and I would guess that many of them had never seen a man who tied solid to the horn.

To appreciate the magnitude of this change, look through the Erwin E. Smith photographs in *Life on the Texas Range* (University of Texas Press, 1973). Smith's photographs, taken on Texas ranches in the early 1900s, show *every* roper tied solid to the horn. A modern photographer, going through the same country today, would likely find just the reverse: every cowboy using the dally method.

Cross-B Ranch, Texas, 1907–1910. A Cross-B cowpuncher branding a maverick in the open range with a ring branding iron. Erwin E. Smith photograph, 1907–1910. *Courtesy of The Erwin E. Smith Collection of the Library of Congress on deposit at the Amon Carter Museum, Fort Worth, Texas. Museum Number LC S6-488.* (Author's note: Taking dallies on such a horn would have been difficult and dangerous.)

For more than a hundred years, cowboys have been arguing about whether the home-end of a rope should be tied solid to the saddle horn or dallied. For what it's worth, no less an authority than Fay Ward believed that "Generally the hand who dallies knows how to handle a rope better than those that always tie" (p. 159). The fact that the argument has gone on for so long and has never resolved itself is a good indication that neither side has a monopoly on good ideas.

It is also an indication that the argument goes a lot deeper and involves a good deal more than what a cowboy does with the end of his rope. The fact is that each method of roping represents a different approach to horsemanship and the handling of livestock. Each is a complete system with its own set of objectives, and those objectives are not necessarily the same. Until this is understood, there will be no peace or communication between the two sides of the argument. When it is understood, both sides should be able to see that the whole argument is rather pointless.

The Hard-and-Fast System

A man who ties solid to the horn gets married to anything he catches. That cold fact determines the kind of horse he chooses to ride and the qualities he tries to bring out in training the horse to respond when something is roped. It also conditions the way the cowboy thinks of an animal he has on the end of his twine. If he can't get away from the brute, he has a tendency to regard it as a threat to his safety, and he will use his horse to subdue it.

The first quality he looks for in his mount will likely be speed. After that, size and strength will be the most important qualities, for his horse will have to be the anchor that will stop, hold, and perhaps trip down whatever he catches, be it a big steer, a crossbred cow weighing 1400 pounds, or even a full-grown herd bull that might tip the scales at 1800-2000 pounds.

Since speed, size, and strength pretty well describe the best qualities of the Quarter Horse, the hard-and-fast cowboy is likely to select a horse of that breeding; with its big chest and hindquarters and its outstanding speed on short sprints. Or, to add a little high octane to the genetic mixture, he might prefer a Quarter Horse/Thoroughbred cross. As Frankie McWhorter once told me, "The only way Thoroughbred blood can hurt you is when it ain't there."

Because in this method of roping the horse functions as an anchor, the cowboy will concentrate on horse training that emphasizes keeping the rope tight at all times. Under the hard-and-fast method, a loose rope is a hazard ninety-five percent of the time, and slack is the enemy. The cowboy can use slack when he's ready to take the rope off and when he flips the rope to lay a trip, but the rest of the time he wants thirty feet of tight rope between himself and his cow. As long as the rope is tight, the cow is under control and horse and rider are safe. Under this training, the horse develops an instinct to move *away* from the cow—to stop, back up, and pull. One that doesn't respond to this training is putting his own safety and that of his rider in jeopardy.

I once heard Stanley Barby, a rancher in Beaver County, Oklahoma, tell about a horse that wouldn't keep the rope tight. To cure him of this bad habit, Stanley tied to the horn, pitched his rope on the biggest cow he could find and stepped off. After the cow had wound the horse up in the rope and jerked him off his feet several times, the horse had learned that the only safe place for him to be was at the end of that rope, moving away from the cow.

Under ideal conditions, the cowboy would also like for his mount to have a soft mouth and a good handle, one that reined well and responded to commands. But these are secondary qualities, the ones he puts on his dream list when he's fantasizing about the perfect pasture horse. If a horse makes a good anchor on the end of a rope that's tied hard-and-fast, the cowboy can forgive a lot of flaws in other areas.

One of the criticisms of the hard-and-fast method is that it can be hard on livestock. Some of my cowboy friends might argue with me about that, but I think it's an unavoidable result of a system in which man and cow are tied together, with no easy way of dissolving the marriage. A man in that situation can't help being aware of it. Either consciously or subconsciously, he perceives the bovine as his enemy. When the cow doesn't cooperate, when he's in a hurry to finish a job, or when he loses his temper, he has a natural tendency to punish the stock. And if he's riding a stout horse that knows how to manhandle a cow and perhaps has developed a taste for it, horse and rider can inflict injury before they realize they've gone too far.

The Dally System

The dally system brings an entirely different set of conditions and concepts to the roping situation, and they all spring from the fact that the cowboy is operating with a loose rope. *That changes everything.* Because he isn't married to his cow "until death do us part," he's more apt to think of livestock as an adversary in a game of skill, rather than an enemy or a health hazard. If things get out of hand, if he loses control of the situation, he simply slacks his dallies, gives his rope to the brute, and rides away.

Some advocates of the hard-and-fast method have taken this as a sign of cowardice, and we'll deal with that charge later on. For now, the important point is that because dallying is a loose-rope system, the cowboy does not have the same mental attitude or set of objectives as the hard-and-fast roper. Although they share the common objective of pursuing the cow to pitch a loop on its horns or neck, at that point, the similarities end. Where the hard-and-fast cowboy stops his horse after making the catch, using it as an anchor, the dally man might or might not want his horse to stop—but he certainly doesn't want him to before the dally is laid around the horn.

With bunch-quitters (outlaw cattle that won't stay in the herd), I usually take a leisurely wrap and ease the cow to a stop, just to let her know that she has come under my control. After she has fought the rope for thirty or forty seconds, I will ride forward, take up the slack, and try to drive her on a loose rope. Other times, I might not dally at all. If I think the animal can be turned around and driven, I will ride forward and try to head her in the direction I want her to go. If she resists, I can always dally up and go to sterner measures, but on many occasions I have managed to drive an animal entirely on a loose rope and never dallied until I was ready to load her into a trailer or to get my rope back.

Slack is not a threat to the dally man. My inclination is to go into a tight-rope situation only as a last resort, and I prefer to handle stock on a rope that is just tight enough to keep my horse from stepping over it with his front legs. Part of one's training in the dally method centers around the controlling of slack, either by maneuvering the horse or by throwing coils into the off-hand. In the case of bunch-quitters, my objective is not to manhandle or subdue, but to persuade the cow to go where she belongs. In the same situation, the hard-and-fast roper would be more apt to slip into a contest of wills and strength—stop, pull, trip, and tie.

Now, there are certain jobs that a dally man can't accomplish on a loose rope—doctoring steers in the pasture or dealing with out-laws that can't be driven. I'm inclined to believe that the dally method is most effective in slack-rope situations and loses its advantages in direct proportion to the tension on the rope. When the dally man has to go to a tight-rope situation, he must compensate for the inherent weaknesses in his system. He has moved into an area better served by the hard-and-fast method. Team roping is one method of compensation. Since the dally man is not as adept at tripping—tripping being one of the major selling points of the tight-rope system—he is more inclined to take down an animal with the aid of a partner who ropes the heels. For that reason, dally men are more likely than hard-and-fast ropers to work in pairs.

Team roping is an excellent method of bedding down stock without inflicting much stress. The only problem arises when a heeler isn't around. When that occurs, the dally man winds his cow up in the rope and pulls her down. Then he throws a half-hitch over his dallies to secure the rope while he goes to the cow and makes his tie. In making this "dally-tie," he has abandoned the loose-rope system and has become a hard-and-fast roper.

It should be obvious by this time that a dally man's horse is not the same as a hard-and-fast roper's. In fact, a mount that is good for one is likely to be a disaster for the other, because they are trained to respond to the same situation in opposite ways. The tight-rope horse is conditioned to stop or turn off once the catch is made, to keep slack out of the rope, and always to move away from the cow unless commanded to do otherwise. The dally horse, on the other hand, is taught to follow the cow once the catch is made, to be prepared to move forward on command, and to maintain communication with the rider at all times.

If I were picking the perfect dally horse—and remember, we're talking about *pasture* work, not arena roping—I would prefer him to be big and strong, but I would give away size to gain mobility and a calm disposition. Mobility is essential in the loose-rope system. A horse that is small achieves this through savvy and quick responses, but one that is slow to react, stubborn, iron-jawed, or hard to turn will cause a dally man nothing but grief. The best dally horse I've ever ridden was a half-Arabian mare named Calypso. When I was using her hard every day, she probably didn't weigh over 950 pounds, if she weighed that. She had cat-hams, a small chest, and long thin legs. At a glance, she seemed a parody of the big, heavily muscled roping horses that can anchor an elephant, and when I rode her on cowboy crews on the Beaver River, I noticed the smirks of the other cowboys. But she had a soft mouth, reined well, responded to spurs, and had a quiet, willing disposition. Riding Calypso, I couldn't jerk stock around, and she had trouble handling the bigger stuff, but we always got the job done. When I missed my dally, she would keep moving and save my bacon.

I would venture to say that in ninety percent of the cases where a dally man loses his rope, it is the fault of the horse, not the man. If he's slow in laying his dally, or even if he misses the horn entirely, the horse can save him by moving *toward* the cow, but when the horse quits moving, sulls, turns away, or backs up, the game is over. Obviously, the dally man should try to avoid riding horses trained in the hard-and-fast method.

So there are the two systems of roping, presented in what I hope is an objective manner. Even though I was trained in the dally method, it's not my intention to propagandize for one side or the other or to add to the bad feelings that have developed between the cowboys and buckaroos. It seems obvious to me that both methods have their place in the livestock business. Why, then, would a man choose one method over the other? Are there some circumstances that would help him, or even force him, to choose between the two?

Although the dally method seems to have become standard on modern ranches in my part of the country, pockets of hard-and-fast roping have remained to the present day, often on big ranches such as the King Ranch, the 6666, and the JA. For years I have puzzled over why the cowboys in one area have embraced the dally method while others, perhaps only a few miles away, have not. Part of the answer might lie in ranch tradition, but I suspect that other factors are also involved. Under certain conditions, which we will examine below, the dally method simply doesn't work as well as the hard-and-fast method, and vice versa.

Terrain

The dally method works best in open country where the roper doesn't have to hurry his throw, and where he has the time and space to handle stock on a loose rope. Give a dally man enough time and space, and he will accomplish his objectives and seldom if ever injure his livestock, his horse, or himself. But put him in canyons, rocks, or heavy brush; force him to rope fast in small clearings; or limit his ability to maneuver his horse, and all at once the fundamentals of dally roping are thrown into stress. At that point the dally man begins missing his wraps and losing his rope, and with loose cattle dragging ropes around the pasture, the cowboy and the dally method begin losing friends.

Buster McLaury, a cowboy who has worked for several prominent ranches and has done some excellent writing on modern cowboying, stressed this point in a *Western Horseman* article. He noted that *all* of the "good" cowboys he has worked with in the brushy country of northwest Texas tied solid to the horn. "A good many of the openings a brush hand gets to rope in are less than fifty feet wide," he wrote, and a man just doesn't have the leisure time to go for his dallies and mess around with slack (p. 12).

When I visited the King Ranch in South Texas in 1982, I heard the same reasoning from Joe Stiles, who grew up working in the brush. I had supposed that since the King Ranch was close to Mexico and had a long tradition of using Hispanic cowboys, their roping techniques would reflect a strong vaquero influence--meaning that they would all be dally men.

Not so, said Joe Stiles. *Nobody* dallied on the King Ranch, neither Anglos nor Hispanics, for the same reasons given by Buster McLaury. Working in heavy brush, you usually get only one shot at a wild cow, and once you catch her, you want to hang on, regardless of the consequences. "Kill thy horse, kill thyself, but rope and hang on."

Frankie McWhorter, who spent three years roping wild cattle out of the mesquite brush in Palo Duro Canyon, told the same story, which leads me to believe that the dally method simply doesn't work as well in heavy brush as does the hard-tie method.

Work Objectives

In September of 1987 I went with Frankie McWhorter to help Larry Dawson gather some wild steers off Dawson's ranch south of Arnett, Oklahoma. They had summered on good grass and weighed around 800 to 900 pounds. They were also very clever at "brushing up" in shinnery motts and eluding cowboys. After the first sweep of the pasture, we came up thirty head short, so we went back and swept the pasture again, this time checking every mott and patch of brush. Those we found were all outlaws and dedicated bunch-quitters, and once we flushed them out of the brush, we didn't give them a chance to lose themselves again. We put a rope on them and tied them down.

I was working beside some fine cowboys and outstanding ropers: Frankie McWhorter and Dan Cockrell of Higgins, Texas; Fred Rule of Elk City, Oklahoma; and Larry Dawson of Arnett. They all tied hard-and-fast and they were all proficient at tripping down big cattle. I was the only dally man on the crew, and this was the first time in thirteen years of cowboying that I had been so thoroughly outnumbered by the boys with the horn loops on their ropes.

I had wondered why they all tied solid, but by the end of the second day I began to realize that the hard-and-fast method simply worked better in this brushy terrain and for this kind of job. When we flushed steers out of the brush, each cowboy picked out a steer and stayed with him until he was caught. At one time we had five men going in five directions. When a man got a clear shot, he had to take it in a hurry and hang on. Taking dallies while dodging brush was an unwelcome distraction, and a missed dally would have turned a wild steer loose in rough country with a rope around his neck. Also, once the steer was caught, the rider often found himself half a mile away from the nearest heeler. He had to trip the beast down and tie him by himself. Tripping heavy stock is a job that can be accomplished much better with a tied rope than with a dallied rope. When the job requires the roper to manhandle his stock, the dally cowboy operates at a big disadvantage.

But the same principle applies in reverse: when the job requires that the cowboy handle stock in a gentle manner, the dally method is by far the better. Precisely because the dally man is handling a loose rope and is always faced with the possibility of losing it, he is reluctant to get himself into a situation where he has to jerk cattle around. Instead of bringing his horse to a sliding stop and flipping the animal over backwards, he will ease into a stop or perhaps not stop at all, choosing instead to drive the animal on a loose rope. When he needs to bed down and tie an animal, he will wait for another cowboy to come along and apply a heel loop, or if he's working alone, wind his rope around the cow's legs and pull her down. Either method is easier on stock than tripping.

Crew

It is hard for a dally man to function well when the other hands on the crew tie solid to the horn. Dally ropers, as I've already noted, tend to work in pairs. For them, team roping is an instinct. If one man goes after a bunch-quitter that is bigger than flanking size—over 400 pounds, let's say—one of his partners on the crew goes with him to heel the animal down.

Cowboys who tie solid and are accustomed to tripping stock don't necessarily have that team-roping instinct. Theirs is a more solitary method of roping, and it might never occur to them to follow another man off into the pasture. In fact, they might even consider it an insult. So the dally cowboy who goes after a big bunch-quitter, assuming that someone will follow him out to back him up, could

One place where the roper, even one who usually dallied in the pasture, might choose to tie solid to the horn is in the branding pen. A tied rope allows the cowboy to concentrate on accuracy and speed without the bother of taking wraps around the horn. *Courtesy of photographer, Sonja Clayton.*

find himself all alone in a big pasture, with no easy way of getting his rope back. Another problem the dally man faces when he's working on an outfit with a hard-and-fast tradition of roping is that the horses are not trained to handle stock on a loose rope. If he rides his own horse, he's okay, but if he rides a ranch horse, he might have problems.

As we've seen, each method of roping has its own approach to horsemanship. A cowboy who ties solid wants his horse to stop when the loop hits the mark. That's exactly what the dally man *doesn't* want, since it throws him into the situation of trying to take wraps with a rope that is burning through the palm of his hand.

Another problem can develop once the cow stops running and fighting the rope. The dally man is apt to slack his dallies, give the cow some air, and go to a loose rope. If the cow decides to run again, the cowboy will spur his horse and follow, still with a loose rope, or take a fast dally. A horse accustomed to dally roping is trained to follow a cow in this situation, but one that has been tied solid all his life backs up and braces himself for a jerk.

When the cow is running forward and the horse is moving backwards, the dally man is in the terrible position of trying to wrap a sizzling hot rope around the saddle horn. At best, he'll lose some skin off his hand. At worst, he'll be dis-roped. In either case, a good dally man can lose his rope and his reputation through no fault of his own, simply because he and the horse were operating under different rules. And that does nothing to enhance the reputation of dally roping on an outfit that didn't believe in it to start with. I suspect that much of the criticism that old-time cowboys directed toward dally roping originated in just these sorts of incidents, when cowboys tried to dally on horses that weren't trained to the system. Naturally, it was a wreck, and the dally method came out looking bad.

We have seen that both methods of roping have their place in the livestock business and that some jobs are performed better with one method than the other. So far, I've kept the discussion on a friendly basis and avoided mentioning the insults that have been lobbed back and forth between the two camps for more than a century. Now let's talk about them.

In *A Thousand Miles of Mustanging*, Ben Green gave a typical Texas cowboy's view of the dally-versus-tie argument:

> I never wrapped and dallied and gave slack when ropin'
> stock. That's the way to lose fingers in the rope and
> that's the way to get your hands rope burned and lose

Little Joe the Wrangler. *Erwin E. Smith photograph, n.d. Courtesy of The Erwin E. Smith Collection of the Library of Congress on deposit at the Amon Carter Museum, Fort Worth, Texas. Museum Number LC S6-367.* (Author's Note: This young cowboy started tying solid to the horn at a tender age. Chances are that he had never seen a dally roper.)

what you've caught, and damn a coward, if you haven't got nerve enough and confidence in your mount to double half-hitch and hard tie, you are going to scar up your hands and lose more stock than you keep. (p. 18)

The important phrase here is "damn a coward." What does dally roping have to do with cowardice? Well, the old-timers just couldn't resist the temptation to equate the dally with lack of courage. My friend Buster McLaury used similar language in a *Western Horseman* article: "If you don't have enough confidence in yourself and your horse to tie on, you've got no business running wild cattle in the first place" (p. 12).

In 1978, when I met Spike Van Cleve, the Montana rancher and author of several fine books, he wasn't quite as blustery as Ben Green, but when he found out I was a dally man, he let me know right away that he had no use at all for the dally. When I injured my back roping cattle on the Beaver River in Oklahoma, he wrote me a get-well note that was pure Spike:

Sorry to hear you are stove up! If you'd 'a been tied hard and fast you wouldn't have had your mind on those damn dallies—and your fingers—and would have been paying attention to what you were doing (namely, popping it on that calf and snatching him over backwards) but I guess if an Okie wants to act like a damn Californero he's got to pay the price. . . . Take care, now, and tie hard and fast and turn off. Imagine an Okie messing with dallies. Mercy! (letter to author, 9 September 1979)

Spike often summed up his thoughts on the subject by saying, "If it's worth catching, it's worth keeping."

With all due respect to these gentlemen of the hard-tie school of roping, I think they have missed the point of the loose-rope system, and are criticizing something they don't really understand. Perhaps what they meant to say was, "In my country and in my work, I don't think the dally method would work as well as the hard-tie method." And I wouldn't argue with that. But this "damn a coward" business is a little hard to take. Anyone who didn't have "nerve" or "confidence" would never be roping in the pasture in the first place, and no dally man I have ever met would argue with Spike's statement that "if it's worth catching, it's worth keeping"—unless keeping the cow required killing or maiming the cowboy, and I know a lot of dally men who would object to that. And so would their wives, children, and insurance companies.

It seems to gall the hard-tie cowboys that a dally man might consider throwing away his rope in a wreck. What's wrong with that? I've done it on several occasions. I never regretted it and I never failed to get my rope back and finish the job. What Ben Green would have dismissed as cowardice seemed pretty good judgment to me. And let's not assume that dally ropers are the only ones who will bail out of a storm. I've seen many a tie-hard cowboy who carried a sharp Buck knife on his belt, instead of in his pocket where I carry mine, and I always suspected that in a wreck, he wouldn't hesitate to whip it out and cut the horn loop out of his rope.

Is a hard-tie man a coward when he cuts himself out of an early funeral? I would wonder about the intelligence of a man who *didn't*. I would bet that when Ben Green was out roping wild stock with his rope tied solid to the horn, he carried a sharp knife on him, and used it on more than one occasion. But don't expect to read about it in his books.

As to Green's comment about a dally man scarring up his hands, missing his wraps, losing fingers, and turning stock loose in the pasture—well, he's got a point there. It happens. Dally ropers do get their hands burned. They do lose cattle when they miss their wraps. And now and then, you meet a man who's missing a thumb or a couple of fingers because he got his hand caught in his dallies.

But against these disadvantages, you have to weigh all the horror stories about cowboys who have been dragged to death, pulled into trees, and even decapitated when they got into a wreck with

COW POKES By Ace Reid

"Well, don't jist stand there
---DO SOMETHIN'!"

Courtesy of Ace Reid Enterprises, Kerrville, Texas.

their ropes tied solid to the horn. J. Frank Dobie told of a Frio County cowboy who lost his head in a roping accident (*A Vaquero of the Brush Country*, p. 104), and in a book called *Southwest*, John Houghton Allen tells of a South Texas vaquero named Felipe who met the same fate (excerpted in *The Texas Breed: A Cowboy Anthology*, Don Hedgpeth, pp. 19-26).

I remember a story Jake Parker told me. It happened up in the Beaver River country, and it still gives me chills. A man had gone out ahorseback to doctor screwworms. Tied solid to the horn, he roped a calf, stepped off his horse, and threw the calf to the ground. But somehow he got into a storm. The calf escaped, the horse spooked and ran, and the cowboy got caught in his own loop. The horse ran back to the house, dragging the cowboy behind him. His wife happened to be outside and saw them coming. When the horse stopped in front of the house, she let out a scream. Battered, bloody, and almost unconscious, he raised up and tried to tell her, "Go to the horse, not to me. *Catch the horse.*" But in her panic, she didn't hear. Instead of walking up to the horse and getting control of his head, she ran to her husband. The horse spooked and ran away, and the poor woman watched as he was dragged to death.

You hear those stories every now and then, and the one common theme in all of them is that the rope was tied solid to the horn. I know a dally man in Oklahoma who doesn't have a thumb on his right hand, but I also met a young fellow from South Texas who lost his entire hand and wrist in a roping accident, when he was tied solid. He is now a good one-armed roper, and he dallies.

The dally roper has to contend with more small accidents and inconveniences than the man who is tied solid, but they don't occur as often as Ben Green has suggested. I have worked with at least two hundred ranch cowboys over the years, most of whom dallied, and I've never known one who was missing a finger or thumb. Most of that amputation business occurs in the arena where the cowboys are dallying for time. They get in a hurry and take too many chances. That's a fault of the man, not of the system. Another place where dally accidents frequently occur is on outfits that don't have a dally tradition, where both men and horses are trained in the tight-rope method and the dally is used only on special occasions.

If you want to know why Ben Green had such a low opinion of the dally method, here's your answer. He was a hard-tie cowboy, riding a hard-tie man's saddle, working in hard-tie country and riding hard-tie horses, and every time he tried to dally, he made a mess of it. He was ignorant of the system he was so quick to criticize.

He probably dallied upside-down and backward on a small steel horn that was never intended for anything but a horn knot. His horse probably ran backwards, just as old Ben had trained him to do, instead of moving forward as a good dally horse would have done. And as a result, Ben probably got rope-burned and lost his cattle. But instead of admitting that he knew next to nothing about the dally method, that he had probably never met a competent dally man or watched one in action, and that he was ignorant, poorly equipped, and poorly mounted for the job—instead of putting the blame where it belonged, *on himself,* he chose to damn all dally ropers and the entire system.

And for every Ben Green on the hard-tie side, you can find an Arnold Rojas who is just as quick to dismiss the hard-tie cowboys as wild, crazy, careless, impatient, bad with horses, and hell on stock. It seems to me that this lack of understanding has characterized the squabble between hard-tie and loose-rope cowboys from the very beginning. Neither side knows enough about the other's methods to understand that each is a complete system, and that you can't move back and forth between them the way you would change hats or boots.

You can change horses, but you can't change the way that horse thinks and reacts. You can change ranches, but you can't change the roping tradition that has been built up and accepted by men, horses, and cattle. You can tie a horn loop into the end of your rope, but that doesn't mean you know how to use it. Cowboys who try, and who use the disasters that follow as a basis for writing off the other guy's method of roping, are doing no service to their profession.

Perhaps we should leave the last word on this subject to Fay Ward, a fellow who knew both sides of the question about as well as any man who ever lived.

> More cowhands have been crippled-up because of tying a rope than by dallying. This should be taken into consideration when doing rope work. Both methods of handlin' a rope have their good points and [are] about stand-off when the subject is really analyzed. A lot depends on the cowhand who is handlin' a rope as to whether it is best to tie or dally. (p. 159)

4

The Evolution of Roping Technique

As we have seen, the Hispanic vaqueros, and the American "buckaroos" who followed them, were a good deal more interested in style than were the cowboys of the plains states. In typical American fashion, the prairie cowboys were in a hurry to get the job done and they had no patience with the vaqueros' habit of playing out a long rope and wearing an animal down. The prairie cowboys preferred to catch and bust an animal down and get on to something else—never mind the style of it.

The differences between the two traditions can be seen in the rodeo events each has produced. The cowboy approach to roping has been institutionalized in the two rodeo events where the rope is tied solid to the horn—calf roping and steer jerking. In both events, the money goes to the fastest time, and style is important only to the extent that it contributes to speed.

The Hispanic approach to rodeo is quite different. At a *charreada*, or Mexican rodeo, contestants in the team roping are awarded points for time but "additional points may be accumulated for the complexity of the twirls of the rope prior to the catch." Furthermore, "a critical element of the *charreada* is adherence to authenticity in dress and conduct" (Carlos Torres, p. 90).

Because the prairie tradition placed so much importance on speed, the cowboy was more inclined to "fairground" and bust cattle than was his counterpart in California. He often did his fairgrounding with a devilish forefooting loop called the Blocker, and it is my belief that in the rise and fall of the Blocker loop, we can follow the dramatic changes that have occurred in ranch roping in the past fifty years. The decline of the Blocker loop is especially revealing, because at one time its use was almost universal. In the May 1940 issue of *The Cattleman*, in a piece called "Ropes and Roping," W. M. French described the Blocker loop.

> The adjective deadly is often attached to the graceful throw known as the "Blocker" . . . said to have been perfected, or at least made famous by John R. Blocker, a Texas cattleman who was one of the greatest of the old trail drivers.
>
> The Blocker is perhaps the most versatile loop of them all. It can be thrown from horseback or from the ground, and it can be used for a head catch, for forefooting, and for heeling from either position.
>
> The Blocker is started in the same way as the straight overhead loop, being taken around the head toward the left. The throw is made when the loop is behind the right shoulder, the right arm being whipped straight forward across the circle it has been describing. At the same time the hand and wrist give the loop a twist toward the left. . . . The loop goes out in front of the thrower, stops, stands up, rolls to the left. . . . In fact, it has turned over. (pp. 23–24)

Chuck King, at one time the editor of *Western Horseman* and a scholar of the roping art, did a piece on the Blocker in the October,

1965 issue of his magazine. As a kid growing up in Wyoming, he knew a man who threw a loop which he called the Johnny Blocker.

> [He] was a hard and fast roper and used quite a bit of loop, but even as an old man he had no trouble jerking the slack out of it. . . . I·am only guessing, but I think the Blocker Loop is Mexican-type roping and could have been a fairly common loop to the good hand with a rope in Old Mexico long before the Blocker brothers made their fame as top ropers. (pp. 52-53)

In my reading of the literature of the cowboy, I have encountered dozens of references to the Blocker loop. Typical is this passage from Ben K. Green's *Wild Cow Tales*: "I was ridin' a good fast gray horse that could sure put me up for a loop at this big set of horns. I pitched a big Blocker loop on him and caught him . . ." (p. 303).

Will Rogers knew the Blocker loop, which he is said to have learned as a boy from his friend Jim Rider. Page 42 of Frank Dean's *Will Rogers' Rope Tricks* shows a photograph of Rogers sitting on a big steer. The captions reads, "This still photograph from [the movie] 'The Roping Fool' shows Will arguing with Big Boy Williams after Will had roped and tied a steer. He roped the steer with a Blocker loop."

Here is another reference to the Blocker, told by Max Coleman in *From Mustanger To Lawyer*. The incident occurred in West Texas, near present-day Lubbock, in the 1890s:

> Standing on his left stirrup, he threw an enormous loop over the steer's right shoulder, catching both forefeet. Just as the steer had all four feet off the ground, his horse tightened the rope, flipping the steer neatly over, a thoroughly chastened and subdued animal. I realized then I was seeing a catch made by the famous Blocker loop that had originated in South Texas. (p. 124)

If the Blocker loop was so good and so versatile, what happened to it? I've worked on ranches in Texas and Oklahoma off and on for twenty-five years, and I've never seen a cowboy throw a Blocker or even heard the name mentioned. "Blocker" is a word I've never encountered outside of a book.

The answer, I suspect, is that at some point between 1900 and 1950 ranch roping in the prairie states underwent some major changes, in response to changes that had occurred in the cattle business. Although, as Mr. French pointed out, the Blocker could be used as a head loop or for heeling, it was used primarily as a forefooting loop. As far as I can tell, it is the only loop ever developed that allowed a man on horseback to forefoot an animal on the run; to put a small loop out in front of the animal, gather up both hocks, and then stand the beast on his nose. That's what the Blocker was designed to do, and back in the days when cattle were wild and cheap, it gave the cowboy a throw he could use to punish rank stock.

One inevitable result of punishing cattle with a rope was a high death loss—broken necks, legs, and shoulders. Frankie McWhorter, who worked on the 500-section JA ranch in the late 1940s, related this experience with forefooting wild cattle:

> From time to time we would forefoot cattle. Coyote Morris taught me how to forefoot. Usually we forefooted just for the heck of it, or if you've got one that runs off and won't stay around the feed ground, you can kind of roll that loop over his withers and head him back.
>
> We crippled quite a few, forefooting. What happens is that you'd start out having both front feet, but by the time you turned off and took out the slack, the loop would be just on that outside foot. It breaks a lot of shoulders. I've quit using it. (p. 37)

Back when cattle were worth $15 a head, that was an acceptable risk. But when ranchers began upgrading their herds with British cattle, they took a dim view of cowboys who drew a crowd of buzzards every time they went to the pasture.

Cowboys from the old school of roping failed to realize that times had changed and that fairgrounding cattle was out of favor. In 1905 the Texas Legislature banned steer roping as a sporting event, and in 1907 steer roping came under a similar attack in Wyoming. In both states, the attack on roping was led by ranchers who maintained that "it was not representative of range-work procedures of the time." In 1923 steer roping was dropped from the list of events at the Calgary Stampede (Fredriksson, pp. 147, 151).

The reaction against steer roping and the decline of the Blocker loop occurred at the same time and were part of the same overall reaction against *all roping*. Had the critics been more articulate, they would have expressed it as a reaction against one particular form of roping: the hurry-up, hard-and-fast, rough-and-tumble methods of the prairie cowboys. It is an undeniable fact that the techniques of the prairie cowboys were harder on stock than those of the West Coast vaqueros. Whether or not the prairie cowboys *intended* to abuse stock is not the issue. The fact is that their approach to roping made it a possibility, and when they were in a hurry, when they lost their temper, when things didn't go as planned, it happened.

If the reaction against the abuses of roping had been more specific, the critics might have suggested that prairie cowboys adopt some of the methods of their counterparts in the West—slow down, learn how to dally, and quit jerking stock around. But that's not the way it happened, and one doubts that those hardheaded old prairie cowboys would have yielded to the suggestion anyway. So what happened was that, in many areas east of the Rockies, there was a general and widespread repudiation of the rope as a ranch tool.

In my book *Cowboy Country*, I told the experiences of an Okla-homa rancher named Stanley Barby. Stanley grew up on the sprawl-ing Barby ranch along the Beaver River, where his grandfather, Otto Barby Sr., disapproved of roping and discouraged his cowboys from doing it. He considered it a tool of last resort, and as a result, the men never had a chance to practice. Roping on the old Barby ranch atro-phied. When the cowboys *had* to rope something, they didn't know how to do the job and often ran an animal to death in their attempts,

Cowboy on the Range Posed His Horse. *Erwin E. Smith photograph, n.d. Courtesy of The Erwin E. Smith Collection of the Library of Congress on deposit at the Amon Carter Museum, Fort Worth, Texas. Museum Number LC S6-122.* (Author's note: In this cowboy's day, cattle were cheap and wild. Horses were small, they were used hard, and they died young. Cowboys tied hard and fast and their Blocker loops left a lot of the bones on the prairie. As the cattle industry changed, so did the ranchers' views of roping.)

which to Grandfather Barby was further proof that the rope was a cattle-killer. According to Stanley, "when he was a boy in the late 1940s, roping was so rare on the ranch that he considered it a major event, and he would ride to the top of the nearest hill so that he could watch" (p. 85).

This repudiation of the rope, made easier by the increased use of corrals and squeeze chutes, plunged ranch roping in the prairie states into a dark age that lasted until the 1950s. During this period much of the roping technology that had accumulated over the previous fifty to seventy-five years simply vanished. As the old-time cowboys died off, their knowledge of loops and throws, including the Blocker, died with them.

As roping fell into disfavor on prairie-state ranches, it moved into the rodeo arena, where it was regarded as a sporting event. If a man wanted to rope, he had to go to town. And there he learned a different way of roping: the dally style used in modern team roping. Until the 1950s, dally roping was virtually unknown on prairie-state ranches, except in states like Montana and Arizona where both traditions had existed side by side. The techniques of dally roping are rather complex and require a good deal of practice. Ranch cowboys had no one to teach them the proper methods and no opportunity to practice, and those who tried to devise their own methods often got themselves into a wreck, which reinforced all the old arguments against the dally—"It's a good way to lose a thumb," and "You get your rope taken away from you."

But then in the 1950s, when ranch roping in the prairie states had reached an all-time low and the old cowboy style of roping had been thoroughly discredited, things began to change. Team roping, a Sunday afternoon sport, moved out of California and into the Plains states. Ranch cowboys, who had forgotten how to rope or had never learned, started going into town on weekends and roping in the arena. They learned how to head and heel, and how to dally the home-end to the saddle horn.

Jake Parker, a cowboy I worked with in the Beaver River country, described the state of ranch roping when he was a young man in Beaver County, Oklahoma:

When I was growing up, nobody dallied. Everybody carried a grass rope and tied it to the horn. I can remember the first dally roping I ever saw in Beaver in the fifties. The local boys were trying to dally for the first time, and they were slow and awkward. They dallied upside down and backward. The dally method was new, and they hadn't learned how to use it.

I think the dally came into use in team roping after the first time dally ropers competed against hard-and-fast ropers at the National Finals Rodeo. The dally ropers beat the tar out of the knot boys, and if you stop and think about it, you can see why. A header who knows how to dally is a lot faster than a header who's tied hard-and-fast. The dally roper only has to deal with fifteen or twenty feet of slack, and if he's good, he can dally on half his rope and get the steer turned in a hurry. The hard-and-fast man has to let the steer go the full thirty feet, and then there is some danger that he'll trip him before the heeler gets there. (*The Modern Cowboy*, p. 100)

That was an interesting turn of events. The buckaroos, who had preserved the dally tradition, were never much interested in speed, but there's no denying that modern team ropers put speed into this dally event. Today, they are so fast that the observer in the stands sometimes gets the feeling that he hasn't seen anything. In a matter of seconds, it's all over. If you want to see what happened, you have to study it on video tape in slow motion. So it was neither the style nor the finesse of dally roping that caught the attention of the prairie cowboys. It was *speed*. If the dally method could win money in the arena, it had to be all right.

It is my opinion, and that of other cowboys I have talked to, that this switch-over from the hard-and-fast method to the dally method was the most important event in the recent history of ranch roping in the prairie states, for when the cowboys had learned the new roping style in the arena, they took it back to the ranches. And when they did, they were better ropers out in the pasture. Using the dally, they were less inclined to trip and bust livestock, and their employers were more inclined to allow roping on their ranches.

When roping fell out of favor on ranches, cowboys had to go to town to learn roping techniques in the arena. From there, the techniques of team roping went out to the ranches and became standard methods. Here, at a ranch rodeo in Albany, Texas, the circle completes itself, as ranch cowboys come to the arena to show off their pasture skills. *Courtesy of Photographer, Sonja Clayton.*

Modern ranch roping, as I observed it during my cowboy career, had become a hybrid that drew from both of the old traditions, buckaroo and cowboy. It was not purely one or the other, but showed the influence of both. From the buckaroo side it took the dally method. From the cowboy side it retained the double-rigged saddle and an emphasis on speed. Purists on both sides probably regard it as a stepchild, but in the parts of the country where I've worked, it has developed into a legitimate style and has become the accepted method of doing business in the pasture. But more important than the purity or nonpurity is the fact that, since the 1950s, ranch roping has made a comeback, and in many areas it has become respectable again to use the rope out in the pasture.

Yet something has been lost in the process. Because the hybrid style uses techniques that were developed in the arena, much of the rich body of roping lore has all but disappeared. There are still ranches that have maintained an unbroken link with the old styles of roping. The bigger the ranch and the more isolated it is, the better the chance that you will find old men who still tie solid to the horn and can throw a Blocker and a hoolihan and maybe five or six other loops.

I predict that in time many of the old loops will be revived and put to use by working cowboys. The arena techniques are good for some jobs, but there are other problems that can't be solved with the standard heading and heeling loops. The Blocker would still be a good loop for the ordinary ranch cowboy and would be an excellent addition to his repertoire.

It would be a shame to lose the techniques developed by those old nineteenth-century cowboys, because they sure as thunder knew what they were doing when they picked up a piece of twine. The next chapter will cover some of the loops and throws that were devised by cowboys many years ago but which have almost disappeared in the present day.

5
Loops and Throws

The standard head-catch I learned in the late 1970s is quite different from the heading techniques described by W. M. French and Fay Ward, the two best authorities on old-time roping. Both French and Ward show the cowboy swinging his rope over his head and around both shoulders. You don't often see that kind of swing today, and when you do, you can bet the roper learned it on a ranch, not in an arena. If you attend an old-timers rodeo, you can see a difference in styles between the cowboys over sixty years of age and those in the forty to fifty age range. Modern heading technique has moved the twirl more in front of the cowboy, to such a degree that his hand and wrist are never out of his line of sight.

I learned my heading technique from a ranch cowboy named Jake Parker, who had learned his in the arena. The points he stressed were: swing the rope in front of you, use elbow and wrist action, point your finger at the target, and dip the loop. Since the old-timers never mentioned "dipping" the loop, we must suppose that they didn't do it. Jake never told me why he dipped his loop, but I have studied

The author in 1980, applying the wisdom of his teacher, Jake Parker: "Swing the rope in front of you, use elbow and wrist action, point your finger, and dip the loop." *Courtesy of photographer, Kris Erickson.*

on it and decided that he did it because we were roping mostly muley (hornless) cattle. To catch a muley animal over the top (as opposed to a side-sweep or ocean wave that comes in from the side), you have to deliver the loop so that the front will drop over his nose. Thus, in dipping the rope, you deliver the loop at an angle, with the front lower than the back.

A cowboy who works around muley cattle is forced to rope the neck. If his cattle are horned, he has a wider selection of throws and can select the one that is just right for the job. He might choose to rope the neck, horns, or half-head. Roping the neck gives him the option of choking the animal down, which is something he can't do with the other two variations. In *The Last Campfire* written by Barney Nelson, West Texas rancher Ted Gray explained one instance when he preferred roping the neck:

> I've doctored lots of bulls, and I've doctored as many as three in one day on the same horse. You need to catch him around the neck instead of the horns, where you can choke him a little until you can get him to stand. If you'll just ride in a circle around that bull about three times and run on the rope, you'll get some feet . . . (and) you can get to him and tie him down. (p. 53)

But while choking a cow might be an advantage in some instances, it's usually not what the cowboy would prefer to do, in which case he will go for a horn catch instead of a neck catch. Instead of dipping his loop and aiming the honda (a small "eye" through which the rope is run to make the loop) at the back of the animal's head, he will give the loop a sideward spin that will pick up the right horn and then fall across the left one. (The process is reversed for left-handed ropers.)

A horn catch will give him more leverage on the cow's neck if he wants to throw a trip on her, and it is also gives him a better handle for pulling. For instance, if he wants to drag the cow into his stock trailer, he doesn't want to choke her down. He wants her on her feet so that she can step into the trailer.

The half-head throw is one I never used myself, and I can't recall that it was ever discussed by cowboys I worked with. It may be a technique that was common in earlier times but which has fallen into disuse in these days of hornless cattle. Frankie McWhorter told me how he used it on bulls on the JA ranch. You'll notice that his technique on bulls was not the same as Ted Gray's:

> We used different kinds of throws on wild cattle, depending on what they were. On bulls we roped half-heads. If you rope a bull by the horns, he'll stand out there at the end of the rope and toss his head around and wear your horse down so he can catch him and kill him. If you rope them by the neck, a lot of times you'll choke 'em to death because you can't get slack into the loop. But if you catch a half-head, you can give it slack. (*Cowboy Fiddler*, p. 37)

Ted Gray mentioned another loop he used on grown cows:

> From experience I learned a better way to tie a big cow, rather than fairgrounding her, tripping her, and breaking a leg or something. I got to roping them old cows over the head with a big loop. I'd let them step through with one foot, either foot, but it was usually the left one because of the way my loop fell. I'd stop that old cow and ride around in front of her and ride off. That foot will come up to her head if you pull her a little ways and she'll fall. (*The Last Camp-fire*, p. 53)

If heading techniques have changed over the years, heeling methods have changed even more. W. M. French and Fay Ward, describing pasture roping methods used prior to about 1940, show the old-time cowboy swinging his heel loop out to the right side, on a *vertical* plane, with the loop coming upward. The loop was delivered *underhanded* at an animal facing the opposite direction from the cowboy. It is hard to believe that at one time underhanded heeling was the accepted method. I have been observing ropers, both on the ranch and in the arena, for many years, and have seen it used only once. But if we accept the words of Ward and French, the underhanded throw was once the most common method of catching heels.

When we compare this throw to the technique used by modern cowboys, we get some feeling for the drastic changes that occurred

This cowboy, at a branding near Albany, Texas, demonstrates the heeling techniques developed by arena ropers. His beef has been head-roped by another cowboy, and he's moving in for the heels. Note the position of his arm and elbow. *Courtesy of photographer, Sonja Clayton.*

once the arena became the training ground of ranch cowboys. The heeling technique used on present-day ranches comes straight from the arena and uses as its model the type of heeling that is done in team roping.

The modern heeler has moved his swing from the side to an overhead position, and delivers his loop on a horizontal, rather than a vertical, plane. He concentrates on keeping his elbow up. He sets up behind the animal or slightly to the left and tries to place the honda of his rope on the animal's right flank. This causes the back side of the loop to stand up and wrap around the animal's back feet. The modern heeler often "feeds" his rope as he swings, increasing its size. This technique not only gives him a bigger loop to work with, but it also allows him to make longer throws than would be possible with a small loop.

We have looked at two methods of heeling out in the pasture, the old-time underhanded throw and the modern team-roping technique. But there are others. One, described by Fay Ward, had a very specific purpose. Out in the pasture, when two cowboys are team-roping grown stock, every now and then they run into a big bull or cow that will sull (refuse to move, or move only in the wrong direction) when roped by the head. If the header's horse isn't stout enough or fresh enough to drag the beast forward, it is impossible for the heeler to make his catch. An animal that is locked down will not step into the loop. The old-time cowboys had this one figured out. Instead of trying to force the cow to conform to a human plan, they adapted their roping style to the will of the beast: laid a big open loop around the animal's hind end and let the brute walk backwards and step into it. Now, that was clever!

The other heeling method is one I saw used by a Hispanic cowboy at a ranch rodeo in Abilene, Texas, in 1988. This fellow, named Pablo, was his ranch's heeler in the team roping event. When the header made his catch, Pablo rode forward until he was abreast of the steer—on the *left* side. Twirling his loop backwards and on a verticle plane, he quickly pitched it under the steer's belly, and did it so smoothly that most of the people in the stands never realized they had just witnessed a very rare type of throw.

As we have said, modern heading and heeling techniques were developed in the roping arena, where they have been perfected by professional ropers who are the best and fastest headers and heelers the world has ever seen. That is the positive side of the shift from ranch to arena. The negative side is the disappearance of much of the old-time roping tradition known to Will Rogers and his generation of cowboys.

In his *Cattleman* article, "Ropes and Roping," W. M. French listed ten or twelve different throws that were known to ranch cowboys of his day. Fay Ward claimed that "the average cowhand is limited to using about six different methods of making a catch" (p. 160). Four of these were horseback loops—the overhead swing, hoolihan, heeling, forefooting (Blocker)—and two were ground loops used for catching horses—the pitch catch and the slip catch.

Of the dozen or more throws used by the old-timers, today's young cowboy is likely to know only the two that came from the arena: heading and heeling. And he might not be aware that there were actually two different categories of roping technique, one for pasture work and one for work inside a herd of cattle.

Herd Loops

Many young ropers of the present day are probably not aware that forty or fifty years ago, ranch cowboys had special techniques that they used for roping inside a herd of cattle, techniques that were quite different from the roping we see in the arena today. Back in those days, a big crew of cowboys would round up a herd in the pasture and drive it to a smooth spot called the roundup ground. Some of the men would be left on the outside to hold the herd, while others dismounted and worked on the ground. Two or three veteran ropers would then change to their best rope horses, ride into the herd, and start pulling out calves and dragging them to the branding fire.

Depending on local tradition, the ropers would either head-rope the calves or heel them, or sometimes use a mixture of the two, heading the little ones and heeling the big ones. If they roped the heads, they used throws that required no twirling of the rope, since

This colt was probably forefooted with one of the horse loops described by Fay Ward, the "pitch catch" or the "slip catch," an essential part of the old-time cowboy's roping lore when horses were wild and cheap. Photo by Chas. J. Belden, Pitchfork, Wyoming, taken in a circular bronc pen of a Northwestern outfit, 1937. *Courtesy of Texas and Southwestern Cattle Raisers Foundation, Fort Worth, Texas.*

the sight and sound of a twirling rope disturbed the cattle and could cause a runaway. I have heard many an old-time cowboy say that any man who rode into a herd and swung a rope above his head would be asked to leave, and he wouldn't be invited to rope again.

This prohibition on twirling a rope in the herd was strictly observed in times and places where the cattle were held out in open country, but I have participated in many old-time brandings where the ropers *did* swing their loops and the matter was never mentioned. The two best heelers I ever saw in a branding pen, Stanley Barby and Glenn Green, used a modified version of the standard arena loop. Fifty years ago, they might have gotten in trouble for that. When I worked with them on the Beaver River in 1978-79, it was never even mentioned.

The reason for this change in attitude lies in the fact that today, most rope-and-drag brandings are held in large pens, not out in the open. Even if the cattle spooked at the rope—and I never noticed that they paid much attention to it—they couldn't escape from the pen.

Hence, the whole matter of twirling a rope in the herd, once considered almost a criminal offense, has taken care of itself in most places, and this has contributed to the decline of the old herd-roping loops. One exception to this is the big 6666 Ranch at Guthrie, Texas. In a piece called "Making a Hand in the 6666 Branding Pen" (*Western Horseman*, July 1984), Buster McLaury made this observation: "*Never* swing your rope over your head as in outside roping. This will scare the calves and make them wild and hard to get close to. Use only the hoolihan loop for calves on your right and in front of you" (p. 60).

When the old-timers necked calves in a herd, they used two throws: the hoolihan (or hoolian) and another which W. M. French called the "overhand toss." The hoolihan toss was known to cowboys of the Traildriving Era (1865–1880) and was mentioned in "Good-by, Old Paint," a song of that period: "I'm ridin' old Paint, I'm leadin' old Dan, / I'm goin' to Montana to throw the hoolihan."

I don't suppose anyone knows where the name "hoolihan" came from. I had always supposed that it was named after some forgotten Irish cowboy, but Paul Patterson of Crane, Texas, who cowboyed in

Lawrence Ellzey, on his horse Happy, loads up a hollihan loop at the 1981 LZ Ranch branding. In 1993, at the age of 82, Lawrence was still necking calves with the hoolihan and still tied solid to the horn. If he ever dallied a rope, he did it behind closed doors. *Courtesy of photographer, Kris Erickson.*

West Texas for many years, has suggested that "hoolihan" was actually a corruption of the Mexican name "Julian," pronounced "Hoo-lee-on" in Spanish (letter to author, 1984). That makes sense because the loop probably originated in Mexico, and we might suppose that some Texas cowboy in the forgotten past learned it from a vaquero named Julian.

Actually, the word "hoolihan" is used to describe two similar throws. What they have in common is that both are swung in a *clockwise* direction, just the opposite of other styles of roping. The first version is a horse loop, used by a man on foot to snag mounts out of a remuda. A right-handed man begins the throw with a large loop lying on the ground on his left side, with his throwing hand just about waist-high. When he's ready to throw, he steps toward the target with his right foot, whips the loop around in front of him, turns it over, and floats it out with the honda on the right side of the loop. The second version is used ahorseback, in a herd-roping situation. Slipping through the herd, the horseman holds a small loop about shoulder-high on his right side. When his shot appears, he gives the loop one quick spin from left to right (clockwise, in otherwords), and flicks it out. Depending on the location of the target, the loop might be delivered on a horizontal or vertical plane.

The hoolihan is a fast loop that can be delivered without warning, and it has the further advantage of decreasing in size as it goes out, which leaves the roper with less slack to handle. Fay Ward wrote that the hoolihan could "be placed in a greater variety of positions than any other method of roping" (*The Cowboy At Work*, p. 160). It can be thrown to the left of the horse's head or to the right. A man who knows how to use it can hit a target anywhere from directly to his off-side to directly behind him, which gives him a range of 315 degrees—a range that can't be approached by any other throw. And, as we have seen, it can be placed in a vertical or horizontal plane.

We might note here in passing that some old-time cowboys used a backward or clockwise twirl for their standard heading loop. In other words, they twirled the rope in the same direction as the hoolihan, but instead of releasing it after one spin, they twirled it several times before making their throw. Perryton, Texas, rancher Lawrence Ellzey told about a man he calf-roped against at a small amateur rodeo in the 1940s. He used the backward twirl in the calf roping, and Lawrence said he did a good job of catching with it.

I remember the first time I ever saw a man throw the overhand toss. It was at a spring branding down on the LZ Ranch, south of Perryton, and Tee Parnell, one of the neighbors, took his turn roping. Tee must have been sixty-five or seventy years old at that time. He'd spent his entire life on the ranch, and had probably never been more than five hundred miles from the place. He was a rare specimen in that he had not been influenced at all by the arena techniques that came out of California in the fifties. He was a living repository of old-time ranch roping techniques, and the loop he used in the branding pen that day was the overhand toss. He would walk his horse through the herd, holding his old grass rope shoulder-high on his right side. Then he would stand up in the stirrups and pitch out a nice soft loop. He threw long and high, giving his loop the arc of an artillery shell, and he seldom missed.

Watching old Tee pluck those calves out of the herd, I thought to myself, "That's so easy, anybody could do it." Then I tried it and found that it wasn't easy at all. Ten years later, I ran into a New Mexico cowboy named Bob Walker who made the same toss, only Bob threw it sidearm, and made it look just as easy—and to this day I still can't throw it well. There's no telling how many calves Tee and Bob necked out of a herd before they could make it look easy.

Buster McLaury spoke of this throw in his piece on the 6666 branding pen:

> If a calf comes by on your left, there's an overhand loop you can use. Bring the loop up over your head and down on the off side in one swift motion. When the loop is released, it should stand up in front of the calf, and he'll run into it. This catch demands split-second timing and is probably one of the most difficult loops to learn. (p. 60)

The overhand toss is a dandy herd loop, but like the hoolihan and the Blocker, it has just about disappeared.

When the old-time cowboys heeled in a herd, they used methods that were not the same as modern arena heeling. An old cowman in Stratford, Texas, once described the difference to me. He said, "Team ropers today rope the heels. We didn't do that in a herd. We *trapped* the heels." To understand the difference between roping and trapping, you need only to watch the heeler at a team roping and imagine what would happen if a man tried it in a herd of cattle. That type of heeling works fine on one animal, but in a herd it would cause a wreck.

This cowboy on the Alexander Ranch near Albany, Texas, has laid a good trap, and as you can see, the other cattle in the herd aren't disturbed about it. *Courtesy of photographer, Sonja Clayton.*

The old-time herd ropers relied on position rather than speed. They were adept at slipping through a bunch of cattle, and when they got into a good position near a calf, they would twirl the rope once or twice and flip a small loop under his belly. This "trap" would stand there while the horse and rider hazed the calf forward. Then the rider would pull his slack, turn his horse, and ride to the fire.

Ted Gray tells about a different type of herd roping, where big steers were team-roped by two Mexican cowboys:

> One of them would ride in there, rope a steer, and drag him up to that fire. The other would pick up his hind feet . . . . Occasionally one of them would pick up the front feet and just ride off with the steer's neck turned back. The other one would pick up his hind feet as he rolled over. It was a masterpiece! (*The Last Campfire*, pp. 40-41)

Barney Nelson saw an ingenius variation of heeling in Montana. When a calf was heeled and dragged up to the fire,

> a piece of rope with a honda and loop was placed around the front two feet of the calf. The piece of rope was attached to an inner tube, which was attached to another piece of rope tied to a stake. When the roper tightened the rope, taking out the slack, the ground crew was free to brand. . . ." ("The Dugan Wagon," p. 41)

I've had the good fortune of working around a few good heelers and watching them work in a herd. They all used a variation of the standard throw—that is, a loop that traveled from right to left. But I've heard old-timers tell about men who caught heels with the Blocker. Paul Patterson of Crane noted: "I used to work with a cowboy, D. J. Wilson of Mertzon, who could throw a heeling loop that would turn over in the air and still fit both heels. Driving cattle, sheep or goats the results were the same—his loop doing a somersault (we used to call it somerset) in the air and still making a catch" (letter to author, 1984). Mr. Patterson's description of the "somerset" loop sounds like the Blocker to me. French notes in his piece on roping: "The Blocker's most common use, perhaps, is as a loop for heeling cattle and it is without an equal for this as it can be thrown from directly behind the animal . . ." (p. 24).

I've never read an account of a cowboy throwing a heel loop out of a hoolihan toss, but I've met several old-timers who knew fellows who did it. Bob Walker told me he'd seen it used in New Mexico, and Frankie McWhorter knew a Mexican cowboy on the JA Ranch who was using it around 1950. Since the momentum of a hoolihan is moving from left to right, the heeler delivers his loop to the left side of the animal, with the honda facing down.

Curt Brummett of Maljamar, New Mexico, grew up around old-time ropers in Eastern New Mexico. When I met him in 1989 he was forty years old, and he knew more about the many variations of the hoolihan than any man I'd ever come across. In a branding pen, he often heeled from the left side with the hoolihan, giving the loop a little flip at the last moment with his first two fingers. He could also catch heels with the same toss, going over the animal's back and bringing the loop under its belly. He had another way of using the hoolihan that I had never seen or heard of before. Facing the east and holding a loop out to his side, he told me to drive his roping steers down the fence behind his back. When the one he wanted came up even with his right shoulder, he flipped out a hoolihan and threw it backwards and underhanded. This was not some kind of exotic throw Curt had dreamed up to impress visitors. It was a good practical loop that he kept in his bag of tricks, and he used it in the branding pen. If the calf didn't offer the kind of position he wanted for a standard toss, he would take what was offered and use the loop that would give him a pair of heels.

Frankie McWhorter insisted that the JA cowboy he had known could catch heels with the hoolihan from either the left *or right side*. I haven't figured out how that could be done. It seems to defy the laws of physics, that a loop moving to the right could somehow reverse itself and go under a calf's belly to the left. But those old-timers were magicians with a rope, and if Frankie says he saw it, he saw it.

Frankie observed another unusual heeling method on the JA Ranch, a throw used by several cowboys of Mexican extraction. These

Good heelers have always been the start of a spring branding, and the best of them have become legends in ranching circles. Two of the best heelers from the Canadian River country in the northwestern Texas Panhandle are Jim Streeter (top photo) and Marshall Cator (bottom photo). *Courtesy of Mr. and Mrs. Jim Streeter.*

were long-rope dally men out of the vaquero tradition who used a maguey rope, made from the fiber of the Mexican maguey plant. The maguey is a very "fast" rope; that is, the loop closes quickly, which makes it ideal for necking horses or small calves. It has a feel similar to that of the modern poly ropes that are popular with calf ropers. But a "fast" rope is no good for heeling because the loop won't stay open or stand up when the roper has laid a trap. Hence, these Mexican cowboys would heel calves by throwing an extra large head loop, letting the calf run through it, and then picking up the heels at the last moment.

I've run across one more heel loop that old-time cowboys used in the branding pen. In the winter of 1984, I was talking to Jim Streeter on the Tandy Ranch along the Canadian River. He described a loop used by Marshall Cator of Sunray, Texas, who, though in his eighties, was still dragging calves on the Lips ranch south of Perryton. Mr. Streeter didn't have a rope in his hands when he told me about the throw, but from his description I was able to go home and work it out on my roping dummy.

What Marshall Cator did was to figure out a way of using the overhand toss, a head loop we've already discussed, as a heel loop. You start out by holding the small loop cocked at shoulder level. When you flick it out with a bit of a sidearm motion, the loop goes straight to the mark, stands up, and wraps around the heels. Jim Streeter, who for years has been known as a great herd heeler, said he never learned to copy the throw, even though he had seen Marshall Cator rope all day with it and miss very few shots. I have heard it said that it took four sets of flankers to keep up with Marshall Cator.

This is just one of many examples of the ingenuity of the old-time cowboys. They didn't learn out of a book. Like Marshall Cator, they felt free to experiment, take a head toss and make a heel loop out of it, and they had the time to play with it and perfect it. If it worked, it was a good loop. What to call it and how to describe it on paper wasn't their concern. There's no telling how many good throws were invented by cowboys on isolated ranches, and died with them.

Any comparison between old-time and modern roping leads to the question of which are/were the better ropers: the old-time ranch cowboys who learned their skills in the pasture or the modern cowboys who have polished their techniques in the arena? It might be silly to raise the question at all since there is no way of proving the case one way or another, but it is just the sort of question that comes up at the end of a day in the branding pen or the roping arena. It seems obvious to me that the old-time ranch cowboy had a broader knowledge of the rope and what it could do than his modern counterpart does. The old-timer knew eight or maybe ten different throws. He could rope heads, horns, heels, or forefeet; cows in the pasture, calves in the branding pen, or horses out of a remuda. And he did it all with one rope, probably a limp old grass thing that a modern cowboy wouldn't use for anything but tying up his dog.

That's pretty impressive. The modern cowboy doesn't know nearly as much about what a rope can do, but in the two throws he has taken as his specialties—the standard team roping loops, heading and heeling—he is probably faster and more efficient than the average old-time ranch cowboy of fifty years ago. If there were some way of arranging a timed event, pitting old-time ranch cowboys mounted on their small mustang-bred horses against modern cowboys mounted on their bigger, faster horses, I think the smart money would go with the modern ropers.

I'd be willing to go a step further and bet that in the United States today, there are more good headers and heelers than at any other time in our history. In my travels around the country, I'm constantly amazed at how many good ropers there are. They gather at little roping arenas every Saturday and Sunday, and if you don't believe they're good, just pull your horse to one of their jackpots and get into it. A time that won money ten years ago doesn't even place today.

Most of these guys (and some gals too) don't work on ranches full-time, yet they raise the level of performance for everyone, and sooner or later it gets back to the ranch. If the ranch cowboy gets humiliated every time he goes to the arena to rope with the town boys, he's going to spend more time on his roping dummy and work harder at polishing his skill.

6
Modern Ranch Roping:
Special Techniques

Roping styles, like styles of dress and speech, come and go. A cowboy who is alert and open to change will pick up innovations wherever he can. At a roundup, branding, bull-cutting, or roping, wherever he comes in contact with other cowboys, he will pay close attention to what the others do and how they use their ropes. If he sees something he likes, he will try it himself. In this manner, roping lore is passed from ranch to ranch, from cowboy to cowboy, across state lines and over a wide area. It results in a kind of standardized body of technique in a particular region. A cowboy takes that basic foundation and then adds his own special techniques as the need arises out in the pasture.

Between 1979 and 1981 I was working on the LZ Ranch in the northern Texas Panhandle. This outfit ran cows and calves year-round, and also had a yearling operation that was pointed toward wheat pasture in the fall and winter. My cowboy partner was a fellow named Tom Ellzey. We did a lot of roping in our work, but we also *studied* roping. We read about it, talked about it, and thought about it. We wanted to be good ropers, and we were constantly looking for ways of adapting our tools and methods to the problems we faced in the pasture. I expect that we were fairly typical of ranch cowboys during this period. We weren't arena-class ropers, in fact neither we nor the horses we rode had ever set foot in an arena. We were strictly ranch cowboys, and everything we did with the rope was directed toward getting a job done.

At any given time, we usually had four or five ropes on hand. My basic pasture rope was a thirty-five foot medium-soft nylon, 7/16 of an inch thick, with a burner made of wrapped baling wire. (A burner is a strip of rawhide, leather, or wire on the honda that prevents the friction of the rope from cutting or wearing away the honda.) Some people might think that a baling wire burner is a sign of a sharecropper outfit, but actually baling wire has several advantages over leather and rawhide—the most obvious being that it is readily available, and the price is right. But there were other advantages as far as we were concerned. It protected the honda better than any material I knew about. It was indestructible; we never had to replace a baling wire burner. Also, it added some weight to the loop, and since we often had to rope in high winds, that little bit of extra weight came in handy. And speaking of wind, I used the 7/16-inch rope for the same reason. I preferred the feel of a thinner rope but I found that out in the pasture the thinner ropes would not carry as well in the wind.

Every rope I kept had its place and purpose. When I bought a new medium-lay rope, I would keep it around the saddle shed for six months or so before I ever carried it on my saddle. I found that a new medium-lay was too stiff for my taste, so any time we did heeling around the corral, I would use it and limber it up. After a while I would start packing it in the pasture. Usually, by that time my previous #1 pasture rope had gotten too limp, and I would begin phasing it out. I kept these old ropes around and used them when I knew we had to pull stock into a trailer. If the old rope got snagged or frayed on a sharp edge, it wasn't much of a loss.

My #1 pasture rope had to be just right—the feel of it, the way it handled and threw. In our kind of work, Tom and I had to go prepared for any kind of roping situation. In the course of a single day, we might have to rope heads or heels on a yearling, horns on a grown cow, or put the twine around the neck of a squirmy little calf. That took in a lot of territory, and ideally a man would choose a different rope for each job: a stiff one for the heeling, a medium or soft one for the heads, and a dish rag for the calf—something that would slop over his neck and hang there. But we had to make one rope do for every situation, so the texture and feel of the rope was very important. My #1 pasture rope had to be soft enough for heading, yet have enough body to stand up in a heeling loop. It had to be light enough to feel comfortable in my hand, but heavy enough to throw into the wind. Under pasture conditions, my rope stayed in prime condition for about three or four months. Then, when it started going limp, making it better for heading but unacceptable for heeling, I would have another medium-lay broken in and ready to use.

When Tom and I knew that we were going out for a big day of roping, usually when we doctored for pinkeye or bloat, we packed two ropes apiece. I had never run into any other cowboys who did this, and I confess that I got the idea from Ben Green, who often carried a second rope. Since that time, I've learned that Buster McLaury used the same trick: "Many a brush popper, when he knows or suspects he'll have to do some roping, will carry an extra catch rope—just in case" ("Brush Cowboy," p. 12).

Carrying two ropes struck me as a smart idea, and the very first time I carried the extra rope, I used it. I was out alone and had to rope and doctor a big sappy steer. I couldn't flank him down and he wouldn't stay on the ground when I tripped him, so I tied the head rope to a tree, heeled him with the second rope, and stretched him out. Another time I came upon a cow that was having trouble delivering her calf. She was horned and in a nasty mood, and she kept trying to fight. I caught her by the horns and tied the rope to the stock trailer, then heeled her with the second rope and bedded her down. With two ropes, I was able to get her under control without busting her and running the risk of killing the calf.

One of the criticisms the hard-and-fast school of roping makes against the dally method is that every once in a while a guy misses his wraps and gets disarmed. Out in the pasture, a lost rope can turn out to be something between a disaster and a catastrophe, especially if you're working alone. In my book *Panhandle Cowboy*, I tell about the day Bill Ellzey and I both lost our ropes and had two wild heifers running through a big pasture in Oklahoma. Ben Green and Spike Van Cleve would have loved that chapter, since it confirms all their darkest suspicions about dally roping.

When you lose your rope, you find out how big a pasture really is. You chase the cow until she stops. You ease out of the saddle and grab the rope, but then she takes off again. You try to throw a wrap around the horn but your horse, who doesn't understand your state of rage and desperation, backs away. You dig your boot heels into the dirt and hang on for dear life. Working together, you and the cow plow a couple of nice lister ridges in the turf before you lose your balance and hit the ground. The cow sleds you through the cactus and sandburs until you finally give up and let go. By this time, your faithful pony has gone back to the house. You're dis-horsed, dis-roped, dishonored, and disgusted. And you still have to get your rope back.

The hard-and-fast boys have a point. Losing your rope in the pasture is no fun. But it needn't be a disaster, if you carry extra ammo tied to the saddle strings behind your cantle. Catching a cow-brute that's dragging a rope isn't easy, but it can be done—and I speak with some authority here, since I've had to do it many times. Instead of following directly behind the animal and getting your horse involved in the dragging rope, you can ride up on the beast's left and make your throw out to the side. Obeying the laws of physics, the loop is inclined to go in a straight line from the bottom of the twirl, so you have to move your swing out to the side and aim it to the side from the very start. Otherwise you will be throwing against the centrifugal force of the loop, which doesn't work too well.

One day in 1979, Tom showed up with a twenty-five foot, 3/16-inch nylon and announced that he was going to carry it as his second rope. I had seen these little ropes in western stores and had assumed that they were toys, something little boys carried around when they played cowboy. Naturally, I scoffed at Tom's idea. But he had done some tall thinking about this, and it turned out that he had a good idea. That little nylon worked slick as a second rope. It was small, light, easy to carry, and easy to tie onto the saddle strings. As a heading rope, its light weight made it harder to throw into a stiff wind than a heavier rope, and it didn't have the body you would want in a prime heeling rope. But it did a good job in the pasture, and it had one further advantage that made it ideal as a second rope. You could use it as a pigging string for tying down grown stock. It gave you twenty-feet of stout, soft cord, and you could wrap up a grown cow like a Christmas present and know that she would still be there when you got back with the trailer.

The first time I discovered this was in the winter of 1980. Tom and I were checking some yearling heifers on wheat pasture and found three of them that were sick and needed to go to the house. We were able to cut them out of the bunch and drive them a mile south to the spot where we had parked the pickup and trailer. But we had a problem: how do two men catch and load *three* heifers without losing one of them? We solved it with that little rope. Tom caught his heifer and held her. I caught mine, wound her up in my catch rope, tripped her down, and then tied her with the little rope. (She was big and stout enough so that she might have broken the little grass pigging string I carried.)

I got my catch rope back and went after the third heifer before she had gotten too far away. I caught her and drove her back to the trailer and was able to haze Tom's heifer from behind while he dragged her in, still holding my heifer at the end of my thirty-foot rope. We loaded mine, then went back for the one that was tied down, loaded her up, and went on our way. That was enough to convince me that

Author John Erickson on the Barby Ranch in Beaver County, Oklahoma in 1979, about to pull a stray heifer into his stock trailer. Trailers have given modern cowboys a degree of mobility never dreamed of by the old-timers, allowing them to use their horses and ropes to great advantage. *Courtesy of photographer, Kris Erickson.*

a "toy" rope isn't necessarily a toy. And for a dally man who doesn't have time to chase his mistakes around the pasture, it can be the best friend a cowboy ever had.

Another technique we used involved the stock trailer. The stock trailer has put wheels under the modern cowboy and his horse, vastly increasing his mobility and giving him a portable catch pen to use in the pasture. After roping an animal, he can drive it to an open trailer, flip his rope over the racks, and drag the animal inside. The stock trailer has become so important to the modern cowboy that it should be regarded as part of his roping equipment. Where the old-time cowboy had to learn certain techniques for roping and tying down stock in big isolated pastures, his modern counterpart has had to master the techniques for dragging stock into a trailer.

When Tom Ellzey and I were cowboying together in the late 1970s, one problem we encountered on a regular basis was roping in high wind. I have read everything I could get my hands on about roping, both old-time and modern, yet I've never found anyone who mentioned this problem. It makes me think that the boys who wrote the books never worked in the Texas Panhandle, or else they suffered a terrible lapse of memory. One day when I was out prowling pastures with Frankie McWhorter in Lipscomb County, I asked him why the old-time cowboys never talked about the wind. He said that when he was working on the JA and Hedgecoke ranches in the late 1940s, they used a 7/16-inch silk manila rope, and he believed that those grass-based ropes carried better in the wind than the modern nylons. If the old-timers didn't mention the problem of roping in the wind, perhaps it was because their ropes performed better than ours.

At the time he told me this, the silk manila rope had become a relic of the past. I had never even seen one, and Frankie could no longer buy them. But he had found a good substitute—a half-inch poly. He said this big rope had just about the same feel as the silk manila, and it carried in the wind better than any modern rope he had come across. This was a *big* heavy rope, and after playing around with it for a while, I asked Frankie if he had to lift weights to strengthen his throwing arm. He laughed and said that, yes, throwing that half-inch poly was about like throwing steel cable. But it did cut the wind, if a guy was man enough to use it.

COW POKES   **By Ace Reid**

"Boy this is some wind, I rope at a calf in front of me and catch a hoss thats behind me!"

Courtesy of Ace Reid Enterprises, Kerrville, Texas.

In the Panhandle, wind is a fact of life. Every day it's out there. Sometimes it loafs along at ten miles an hour, but it's just as likely to be blowing twenty-five or thirty. It doesn't take much wind to mess up a roping party. If your horse is running at thirty miles an hour, you've already got that much wind resistance working against you. Add another twenty or thirty miles an hour to that and you've got problems. Wind can have a disastrous effect on a head loop. The style and technique developed in practice sessions come to nothing in a wind. This is one roping problem that can't be solved on the dummy, since you can't reproduce the effects of a fifty-mile-an-hour wind. If you make your normal throw into a high wind, the loop will never get there. It will either die in the air and land on the animal's back, or it will fold up, turn and flutter into the dirt like a gutted sparrow. In the Panhandle, if you don't find a way of correcting this problem, you will become an expert cusser but a poor pasture roper.

Tom and I tried several corrective measures. We went to heavier ropes and bigger loops. We made our burners out of baling wire, which added some weight. We tried moving our hand-hold farther down the rope from the honda, which also added some weight. These methods helped, but they weren't good enough.

I tried to come up with a different heading style, one especially suited for roping in high wind. Modern heading technique, which has the loop swung in front of the roper, is very accurate. By delivering the loop out in front, as opposed to bringing it over your head, you reduce the chance for error and miscalculation simply by reducing the length of your swing. But this style has one major disadvantage: unless you have a very strong throwing arm, you can't deliver the loop with enough force to overcome the resistance of a high wind. It's the difference between throwing a dart and throwing a baseball. The old-time cowboy who took a big wide swing over his head and used his entire arm and shoulder gave away some accuracy, but he could throw harder against the wind—which might be another reason why the old-timers never mentioned the wind problem. I tried that method, swinging with the whole arm, just raring back and throwing as hard as I could. But what I gained in distance I lost in accuracy. It doesn't do much good to get the loop out there if it doesn't hit the target.

When all else fails, a guy should try the simplest solution. That's what Tom and I did. It finally occurred to us that we should start approaching our stock from the windward side and making our runs with the wind. If the cattle circled back into the wind, we would hold our fire and wait until we had the wind to our backs again. At first it seemed that this method was too slow, that we were running the stock too hard and wasting time and energy waiting for a good shot.

But it wasn't slow, not when we could nail the cow on the first loop. What's slow in the pasture is throwing loops into the dirt and then reloading. By using a little patience, we were able to do our pasture work better and faster, and we cut our use of profanity in half.

Another technique Tom and I added to our repertoire was what you might call the "pasture herd shot." We used it mostly in the summer when, of an afternoon, the cattle would bunch up around a windmill or waterhole. Riding through them, we could oftentimes catch sick calves where they stood, without having to run them. Any time we could avoid running an animal, we did it.

Herd roping in the pasture requires finesse, cunning, and a minimum of movement. The most common herd throw is the hoolihan, the quiet toss made with one clockwise twirl of the rope. I often went to it for my pasture herd roping, though I was never able to throw it with the same degree of confidence that I had in my standard head shot. Its one big advantage is that you can deliver it to the left, to the front, to the right, or even behind you. You don't have that wide a range with a loop that is swung several times, since the swing creates a centrifugal force that limits your throwing radius.

Tom didn't care much for the hoolihan, even though he had grown up on a ranch where his father, Lawrence Ellzey, used it a lot and was good with it. Tom carried a thirty-five-foot rope (which was considered long in our country), and he had enough strength in his arm to throw to the end of it. On the roping dummy, he would practice making throws that most cowboys considered impossible, throwing the entire length of his twine, minus a couple of feet for the loop. When we got into contests on the dummy, he could usually beat me with this long throw. Out in the pasture, around a waterhole, Tom would build a small loop, swing it one time, and let it fly. I've seen him snag cattle that were so far away from him that they didn't even know he was there. By the time the animal got the news, Tom had already made his catch and dallied the last foot of rope around the horn.

There was another pasture problem that we gave us trouble. Every once in a while we would come up against an animal that ran with his head down, and if he was hornless the problem was compounded. Even a perfect throw passed over the head and hit the dirt. Muley bulls, such as Brangus, are perhaps the most difficult of all targets for a cowboy using the conventional head shot. Not only will he run with his head down, but the hump on his shoulder creates a natural barrier to a normally-thrown loop.

I would bet there are cowboys around who have come up with a technique that will work on a "headless" target. It may involve hazing the animal off to the right and then coming around with a "sidesweep" or an "ocean wave," delivered sidearm, that puts the loop in a vertical rather than horizontal position. With the loop standing straight up, the beast runs into it as he veers off.

I once ran into a cowboy from Lipscomb County, Texas, who had his own solution to this problem. When he roped in the pasture, he *heeled* everything on the run. He had developed this technique while working alone and found that he could take down big cattle better with double-hocks than with a head catch. That saved him the trouble of having to trip the beast and tie him down. And of course it didn't matter to him if the animal ran with his head up, down, or sideways. I've never tried this approach, but I think it would be a good one. It solves a lot of problems for the man who is working alone, and it shows what a cowboy can come up with when he uses his head and applies common sense to a pasture problem.

Frankie McWhorter told me about a special technique he has used on bunch-quitters:

> You build a little loop and drop it over his behind as you ride past, and then take a short dally. It turns them over and it sounds like it's breaking every bone in their body, but it's sure good for bunch-quitters.

This, of course, is a variation of the old Mexican trick of "tailing" an animal down, where the cowboy grabs the tail, dallies it around the horn, and then turns off, throwing the beast head over heels.

Any cowboy who does much roping in the pasture will encounter problems that can't be solved with the standard head shot or heel shot. When that happens, he must fall back on an ancient bit of wisdom: If at first you don't succeed, get a bigger hammer. Or try a different loop. Why not? There may be certain accepted rules for roping in arena competition, but out in the pasture what's *good* is whatever works.

7

Roping on Wheat Pasture

 n his book *The American Cowboy in Life and Legend,* Bart McDowell quoted a modern rancher who was antagonistic toward ropes and ropers. "We do no cowboying here. We don't even permit ropes on the saddles. If we find an animal that needs attention, we bring it up to the house and use a squeeze chute" (p. 29). Many ranchers share this fellow's opinion that the rope is a crude, old-fashioned tool that belongs in the roping arena, not on a streamlined cattle outfit devoted to bottom-line economics.

On some outfits, the squeeze chute approach works fine. If the pastures are small, if the cattle are docile, and if you don't have to go far to find a set of corrals, a squeeze chute can take care of most of the problems that come up—although having worked both chute and rope, I still maintain that the squeeze chute has smashed more fingers, broken more jaws, knocked out more teeth, and taken more hide off men and animals than any other device invented by man. The squeeze chute has its place, but where ideal conditions don't exist, it doesn't work so well. Perhaps the best example of this type of situation is the modern wheat pasture operation on the High Plains of Texas, Oklahoma, and Kansas.

Running cattle on wheat pasture during the late fall, winter, and early spring presents the modern cowboy with a unique set of problems which are quite different from those encountered on a grass-pasture operation. Wheat pasture cattle are likely to be young, silly, and vulnerable to a wide variety of health problems. They are likely to be strung out over a wide area. Since wheat pasturing is a seasonal enterprise, fencing is temporary, usually a one-strand electric fence, and working corrals consist of whatever you can cobble up out of a trailerload of portable panels. On a normal day, a wheat pasture cowboy might drive seventy-five to one hundred miles to check on five hundred to one thousand yearlings, located anywhere from two to seven places. If he finds sick cattle, he can spend half a day moving up corral panels and a squeeze chute.

Or he can dispose of the problem in minutes through the skillful use of the catch rope. It appears to me that there is no segment of the cattle business that lends itself quite as well to roping as the wheat pasture operation. A cowboy who is well mounted and knowledgeable about roping can take care of any problem that comes up. When you figure the bottom line—cowboy labor versus wear and tear on pickups, the cost of corrals and chutes, the time spent setting them up, and death loss—roping skill translates into dollars saved.

When I was working for the Ellzeys, we began receiving fresh cattle in the early fall. We held them on grass for a few months while we cleaned them up and got them straightened out. Then, around Thanksgiving, we moved them up on the flats to wheat and stalk fields. They stayed there until the middle of March, or longer if we had graze-out wheat. While they were on wheat, Tom Ellzey and I tried to ride through them at least once a week. Sometimes only one of us could get free to do the prowling, but most of the time we worked as a team.

In the fall our major problem was sickness: pneumonia and scours. In the spring, when warm days caused the wheat to grow rapidly, we were faced with that dreadful malady, bloat, which can kill steers about as fast as anything you can name. And no matter

Jake Parker and the author team-roped this bloated heifer on wheat pasture. Jake, a deadly roper in the pasture who would smear his loop on anything with hair on it, is shown running a rubber hose into her stomach to release the buildup of gas. Taken at the Three Cross Ranch, Beaver County, Oklahoma, 1978. *Courtesy of photographer, Kris Erickson.*

what the season, fall, winter, or spring, we had to doctor for pinkeye. On a typical day, we would load our two horses into a sixteen-foot stock trailer and spend the day going from pasture to pasture. We carried neither corral panels nor squeeze chute. In the pickup or on our persons, we packed pinkeye medicine, antibiotics, and a rubber hose for letting down bloaters.

We left the pickup and trailer just inside the wheat field, parked it in a position that wouldn't allow the wind to blow the trailer gate shut, and left the trailer gate open so that if we needed to take an animal home, we could load him without getting off our horses. Then we would split up and count the cattle. On the back side of the field, we would get our tally straight and then ride back through the herd, looking for dropped ears, bad eyes, dirty tails, dry noses, and so forth.

We had a system worked out for our team roping. Before we started a run, we had assigned the heading job to one man, or at least we had decided who would make the first throw. Usually this was determined by the horseflesh. If one of us was mounted on a green colt or a slow horse, the other man roped the head. If the header made his catch on the first loop, the trailing man moved in and scooped up the heels. If the header missed his loop, the trailing man galloped in and took over the heading job.

The trailing rider also served as a lookout and hazer. In the heat of a chase, the header's attention was focused on his roping: the feel of the rope and the location of the steer's head. Accurate roping requires intense concentration and the roper tends to lose track of where he is and where he is going. On wheat pasture, that can lead to problems. Before you know it you can run a steer through an electric fence which, unlike a good honest barbed wire fence, is hard to see. Or, God forbid, you can run your *horse* into an electric fence, which is a subject of cowboy nightmares. A horse that has gotten into an electric fence will go nuts, and for the rest of his life, when he sees a strand of wire on a steel post, he will remember that bad experience. It was the trailing man's job to scout the country ahead and to *know* at all times where the fences were. When he saw a fence com-

Author heading on Calypso, and Tom Ellzey heeling on Happy, on wheat pasture near Perryton, Texas, 1980. *Courtesy of photographer, Kris Erickson.*

ing up, he would warn the header and then try to haze the steer in another direction.

We always started our runs with the wind and made our throws with the wind to our backs. But sometimes the steer would try to loop back to the herd, into the wind. The trailing man would see this coming and move in to haze the steer out of the wind.

Finally, the trailing man served as a kind of roping critic. He watched the header's style and technique. If one of us was having a bad day, he would say, "Watch me and tell me what I'm doing wrong." We knew each other's style, including bad habits and wrong tendencies. My most common problem was throwing beyond my range. I was most accurate about ten feet away, and when I threw longer, going for a quick catch, my loop fell to pieces. I was also vulnerable to sucker shots, throwing at a steer that hadn't lined out and started running straight. Tom's most common problem came when he slipped back into his old habit of swinging the loop above his head, instead of out in front. This caused him to whip the loop at the last second, making it tumble in the air.

While we doctored most pinkeyes on the spot, we always took sick cattle back to the ranch. We would catch them as quickly and quietly as we could, then drive them on a loose rope to the trailer. There, the roper would throw his twine over the racks and haul the beast toward the gate, while the second man dismounted and assisted afoot. Occasionally, with heavy stock, we had to fit the animal with a nylon halter and winch him in with come-alongs, which are hand-operated winches most cowboys carry with them in their pickups. One way or another, we got him loaded.

In the case of bloaters, we always took them off wheat and back to grass, reasoning that if they bloated once, they could do it again. We marked them with ear tags so that we wouldn't take them back to wheat. If the bloater was obviously in bad shape, we treated him on the spot, running the rubber hose into his stomach and letting off the trapped gas. In the two seasons that Tom and I maintained our "bloat patrol," we didn't lose a single wheat pasture steer to bloat. The evidence in other fields around us and in the borrow ditches suggested that other outfits didn't enjoy the same success.

The squeeze chute is fine where you can use it, but on wheat pasture it's hard to beat a couple of good cowboys who know how to use that old fashioned tool, the catch rope.

8
Doctoring Pinkeye

Back in the early 1960s, when I was a high school kid working summers on the Flowers Ranch, I didn't see many cases of pinkeye. At that time the prevailing wisdom held that pinkeye was an affliction of Hereford and white-faced cattle ("Black cattle don't get pinkeye," we often said), and it was strictly a summertime problem. Nobody was sure what caused it: sunlight, pollen, flies, germs, a virus or a combination of these. We didn't worry much about it and we didn't doctor it very often. When we did, we used crystal violet dye—"blue drops," we called it—and you could always tell when a man had been doctoring pinkeye. He had blue fingers for the next two weeks.

In 1978, when I was cowboying on the Beaver River in the Oklahoma Panhandle, I got my first experience doctoring pinkeye on a regular basis. I was looking after a herd of mostly Hereford cattle. We had pinkeye problems, and the boss gave me orders to doctor it in the pasture, when and where I found it. Between April and October, I prowled my pastures twice a week, and most days I roped and doctored anywhere from two to eight calves. Now and then I would find a cow or a bull with pinkeye, but since I was working alone and

Tom Ellzey and the author doctoring pinkeye on the flats near Perryton. Once we had the steer on the ground, we put the head rope around the front hocks so that our critter was stretched out and immobilized. Note the little bag on my belt, which we used to carry medicine and eye patches. *Courtesy of photographer, Kris Erickson.*

wasn't too keen on pitching my loop on big stuff that might not want to give my rope back, I didn't treat adult animals unless they went crippled in both eyes. On this outfit, I used the old-time treatment. I carried a small bag of stock salt on my belt and threw salt into the bad eyes.

Salt seemed to work as well as the blue drops—I had never been convinced that the violet dye did much good anyway—and we didn't have any calves stone blind at shipping time. An old cowboy once let me in on a variation of the salt remedy. Back in the old days, he explained, if a cowboy found a bad-eyed calf out in the pasture and he wasn't carrying salt, he would use what he had on hand. He would urinate into the eye, and the salt in his urine would help heal it. I never tried it so I can't say if it worked or not.

In 1979 I went to work for a yearling outfit in Texas, and while I was there I learned more than I ever wanted to know about pink-eye. It was a scourge. We fought it all the time. Among the things I learned was that the old rules I had heard as a lad just weren't true. Black cattle, or at least black yearling cattle, *can* get pinkeye, and when they do, it's likely to be a bad case since you can't see the first symptoms as well in black-faced animals as in white-faced. I also found that among yearlings, pinkeye doesn't know summer from winter. We fought it year-round.

In his book, *The Stockman's Handbook*, Dr. M. E. Ensminger says that "keratitis" (pinkeye) is an infection caused by the bacteria *Moraxella bovis*, and can be brought on by "vitamin A deficiency, injuries, dust, insects or strong sunlight." He points out that pinkeye "does not usually occur in the winter months" (heh, heh), and for treatment he recommends that you lock the affected animals up in a dark stall and "call the veterinarian." It is comforting to know that we had a scientific name for pinkeye and that if a guy ran into "keratitis" in the pasture he should call the vet. Comforting, but not very practical. If I had called the vet every time I found a case of pinkeye, I would have bankrupted several of the outfits I worked for. The working cowboy has to be his own vet and come up with his own treatment. And if he looks after hundreds or thousands of animals, his treatment has to be something other than locking the pinkeyes up in a dark stall. Even in Texas, they don't make barns that big.

During my cowboy career, I went through several patent medicines, powders and potions, but what seemed to work the best was one that Tom Ellzey and I used on yearlings. This treatment started with the long arm of the cowboy, the catch rope. Working as a team, we rode through yearlings and looked for bad eyes. In the summer we did this in ranch country; in the fall and winter we prowled on wheat pasture. When we found a bad-eyed steer, we team-roped him and stretched him out, with one horse holding both hind legs and the other holding both front legs. Stretched out in this way, a steer wasn't able to struggle or throw his head against the ground. One of us would slip a small-gauge needle under the white of the eye and inject 2 cc's of a half-and-half mixture of cortisone and penicillin, which formed a bubble under the tissue. At the same time, the other man was preparing an eye patch.

You can buy rubber eye patches at the vet supply store, and they work very well. But if you are doctoring a large number of animals, as we were, your eye patch bill runs up in a hurry. We used patches of cloth—clean grease rags, last year's blue jeans, just about any kind of heavy cloth material. We cut the cloth into patches, about 4" x 4," and stuck them over the animal's eye with eye-patch glue that we carried it with us. The patch would hold for a couple of weeks, protecting the eye from light, flies, pollen, and branches, and by the time it fell off, the eye had usually healed. I don't know whether the medicine helped, but I'm sure the eye patches did. Patching is a sensible, practical way of protecting the eye and giving it time to heal. It accomplishes what you would get if you locked an animal in a dark stall, and the interest payments on an eye patch are a good deal cheaper than the interest on a new barn.

Roping bad-eyed cattle in the pasture is, as they say, a different sack of cats. Your approach and techniques are not the same as those you would use against cattle with good vision, and this is one area of pasture roping that can't be learned in the arena. In fact, arena roping might even be considered bad preparation, since the emphasis there is on speed. With blind and half-blind stock, speed is dangerous, and your first rule is always caution. You never know what a blind animal is going to do or where he will go. He's completely unpredictable, for the simple reason that he can't see you, your horse, or the country ahead. In the worst cases, he's navigating strictly by sound. He might run straight or he might dodge. He might cut suddenly in front of your horse. Or, when you're up in the stirrups and ready to throw, he might stumble and fall.

One time I found a blind calf in the pasture. He had lost his mother and was walking around in circles. He was dehydrated and starving to death, and I had to do something with him. Driving him was difficult since he couldn't see my horse. I had to rope him. Just as I was about to make my toss, he cut to the right, stepped off a twenty-foot cliff, and fell straight into the creek below. For a minute or so, I didn't have time to worry about his health because my horse, a pretty good kind of bird-dogging horse that followed cattle well, tried to go off the cliff behind him. The fall could have killed or crippled the calf, but he was lucky. It didn't seem to bother him at all. I finally got a rope on him, tied him down, and came back later with the stock trailer and took him to headquarters. We patched both eyes, got some water down him, and the next day took him back to the pasture and found his mother. He was blind until the eye patches fell off several weeks later, but he stayed with his mama and continued to nurse.

I have talked with ranchers and even veterinarians who told me that their solution to pinkeye was to leave it alone. They never doctored it. But how could you not doctor a case like this one? If we had left the calf alone, his mother's bag would have swelled so that he couldn't have gotten any milk, even if he'd been able to find her. Eventually she would have gone dry and the calf would have either died or been a runt for the rest of his life. If you're running a purebred herd and you want nature to weed out the animals that have a weakness to eye problems, okay—don't rope, don't patch, don't doctor. But if you're looking after commercial cattle and operating on a thin margin to start with, then you take care of calves that go blind. I think ranchers who never doctor pinkeye have never ridden up on a calf that was lost, blind, and walking in circles.

On another occasion I found a calf that had two bad eyes, and he was off by himself in a corner of the pasture. As usual, I approached him with caution and tried to slip up and get a loop on him before he ran. But when he heard me coming, he turned and ran— straight toward a fence that he couldn't see. I spurred my horse and went after him, knowing that if he got through the fence, he would be in the neighbor's pasture and I'd spend the rest of the day trying to find him and bring him back home. I built to him but not fast enough. He hit the fence and went through. The middle wire tripped him, and while he was getting back on his feet, I made my throw across the fence. It went straight and true and I caught him.

If he'd been a bigger calf, I would have been in a mess. My horse would have boogered at the wire, and I would have either been bucked off into the fence or else thrown my rope away and lost everything. But he was small enough so that I could hold him without the horse. I got down, pulled him through the fence, doctored his eyes, and let him go. And my mare was kind enough to stand ground-tied through it all and give me a ride back home. But this story is another illustration of how you can't predict what blind cattle are going to do, and how you can get yourself into trouble roping them.

Up on the LD Bar in Oklahoma, I used to ride a bay horse named Little John. He'd been trained in the arena before I got him, and he was fast, chargy, and aggressive. He would go after a calf as though he intended to eat him, and he would sure enough give you good close shots. That was fine for the arena, and it was fine when we went after cattle that could see. But when we doctored pinkeye, that horse scared me to death. He had no pasture savvy, no caution. I guess he'd never had a blind calf run under his legs and roll him up. Although he was the best roping horse on the ranch, I rarely used him for doctoring pinkeye.

My best doctoring horse was a big old lazy sorrel Quarter horse named Star. He would have starved you to death in the arena, but he took care of you in the pasture. He savvied blind stock, and he never got close enough to get tangled up in one. A guy had to throw long on Star, but that was all right with me. Throwing long is a good strategy to use against blind stock, since distance is your best protection against a wreck. I've seen blind cattle that started out running straight, then suddenly changed directions for no apparent reason. Later, I figured out what had caused it. The animal, going strictly on sound, had picked up the echo of its own footsteps, bounced off a big cottonwood tree or a creek bank. Its natural instinct was to dodge away from the sound.

Another strategy I used on blind stock, and one I preferred, was the sneak attack. Don't give the little brute a chance to run. Slip up on him and nail him in his tracks. This method works best around a waterhole in the summer, when the herd is lazy and doesn't want to run. You can ride around and through the herd and ease up to the one you want. The hoolihan is good in this situation. If the calf is blind in one eye, you can sometimes slip up on the blind side and nail him, though one-eyed cattle are pretty cagey about that blind side. They are easy to spot in a herd because they have to turn their whole head or body to watch you, and they often face you with their head cocked at an angle.

But even the sneak attack has its hazards. One winter Tom Ellzey and I found a 400-pound steer that was as blind as a brick. (He was one of those good blacks that don't get pinkeye.) We eased into the herd, one man on each side, and waited for a good clean shot to develop. He came my way, and when the shot developed, I swung once and floated out a nice soft loop that hit the mark. When the steer felt the loop close around his neck, he exploded. He ran to the end of the rope, and just as I dallied on the last six inches, he leaped high in the air and hit the ground on his back. Then he was on his feet and running straight for my horse. All at once I had thirty feet of slack for my horse to step into and a blind steer that was trying to go between his legs.

I got my horse out of the way and out of the rope just in time to take a shorter dally and throw the steer again. He bounced up and came toward me again, this time leaping like a deer. I had never seen a steer behave this way. There was no pattern to his movement, no way of predicting where he would go next and no way that Tom could get a heel rope on him. I turned my horse, spurred the hair off him, and dragged the steer around until he fell down. When his back

These cowboys on the J. Y. Crum Ranch are painting the navel of a newborn calf to protect it from screwworms, which were a plague on the cattle industry. Photo by James Cathey of Fort Worth, 1950s. *Courtesy of Texas and Southwestern Cattle Raisers Foundation, Fort Worth, Texas.*

legs went up into the air, Tom was right behind me and heeled him on the ground. We got him loaded in the trailer and took him home, but we'd earned our wages that day.

I've heard old-timers say that pinkeye is worse today than it used to be, and I expect they're right. I've noticed, for example, that while old-time cowboys often mention the problem they used to have with screwworms, they don't say much about pinkeye. And in my readings on early-day ranching, I can't remember a single reference to pinkeye. It could be that pinkeye is more of a problem today because cattle are moved around so much. A modern yearling operation handles shipped-in southern cattle that have spent time in sale barns, trader pens, and cattle trucks, and it would make sense that they are more likely to develop eye problems than native cattle on grass. But even native cattle seem to get more pinkeye today than they did twenty years ago.

Eventually somebody will come up with a sure-fire method of controlling it, or maybe somebody already has and I don't know about it. But where I've worked, the best cure for pinkeye has always been an alert cowboy, riding his pastures on a regular basis and using his catch rope to save the boss some money.

9
The Rope as a Weapon

The purpose of the catch rope is to catch. That's why most of us carry it on the saddle with us. But even if a man isn't a good catcher—"a hoper instead of a roper," as they say—it's not a bad idea to carry a rope anyway.

As noted in Chapter One, the Mexicans, Persians, and Mongols sometimes used their ropes as weapons in battle to unhorse and even dispatch an adversary. The average cowboy shouldn't find too many opportunities to use his rope against humans, but he can sure use it as a weapon to protect himself against certain animals.

A catch rope is the all-time best rattlesnake killer on the market. With a little practice, a guy can learn to swing the honda and hit a small target at a safe distance of seven or eight feet. You wouldn't think that little knot would hurt anything, but give it a good swing at the end of ten feet of rope and it will dispatch a snake in short order. You can smash a rattlesnake's head with one direct hit—and I've done it.

I've also thought that a rope could provide an excellent cure for a biting dog, the main reason being that I've never been around a dog that wasn't afraid of a rope, once he was introduced to it. I've never tested my theory on one that was serious, but if I ever got the chance, here's what I'd do. If the dog showed bad intentions but kept his distance, I would shake out a medium-sized loop and try to catch him loose—that is, I wouldn't want to zip up the loop and hold him, since that would present the problem of how to get my rope back. I would just want to demonstrate that I could reach him, in spite of the distance between us, and that if I wanted to catch him for keeps, I could do it. Unless he were particularly vicious and trained to hurt someone, I think the shock of that realization would be enough to send him under the house or to a distant corner. But if he came at me, I would slide the loop out of the rope and use the rattlesnake-killing technique. After I'd whacked him across the nose, I have an idea that he'd change his mind about biting me. Any dog that kept coming at that point would lose his rating as a pet. I would then try to pitch a small loop on his neck and either choke him down or carry him by the neck to his master.

On the drag-end of a herd, you can use the rope to spank slow-moving cattle. If you know how to use the knot-end, you can reach out and pop a snorty bull right on the end of his nose, and maybe discourage him from taking a razoo at your horse.

There's another type of situation in which you can use your rope as a weapon: when you're riding a mare and get attacked by a stud horse. In the fall of 1978 I was working on a big roundup crew in the Beaver River country. It was shipping time and we were gathering all of Stanley Barby's pastures, sorting up the cattle and moving them into traps near his shipping pens. A crew of fifteen cowboys gathered the animals from one pasture, and when we got them penned Stanley told me to trailer my horse over to another pasture, jump out on the south end, and start pushing everything north. When the crew finished sorting, they would join me. Then, with a grin on his face, he added, "Oh, and you might keep your eyes open. There's a band of mares in that pasture, and a stud horse. He might try to climb into the saddle with you." I was riding a mare, you see.

Shoe Bar Ranch, Texas, 1901–1910. The boy wrangler for the Shoe Bar brings in a load of wood; the cowboy's favorite method of "totin'" things. *Ervin E. Smith photo, 1901–1910. Courtesy of The Ervin E. Smith Collection of the Library of Congress on deposit at the Amon Carter Museum. Museum Number LC S6-886.*

By the time I jumped Calypso out on the south end of the pasture, it was misting rain and a heavy fog had moved in. I could see maybe twenty-five yards and that was it. I hoped that the stud horse couldn't see any better than I could. I loped out the south end and started the cattle moving north into the rain. I tried to keep my glasses wiped clean, but within minutes they were fogged and wet again. The minutes dragged by. Half an hour passed, then an hour. No stud horse. My mind began to wander, as I thought about how cold and wet I was.

I had just about decided to coil up my rope and tie it back on the horn string when I heard the pounding of hooves and the snapping of brush. I couldn't see the son of a gun but I could hear him, and in that fog it sounded like a whole herd of stud horses coming after me. I turned and faced the sound, yelled, and started swinging my rope. He came out of the fog and stopped. He snorted and squealed and stamped his feet at me, and in the sternest voice I could muster, I gave him to understand that if he came one step closer, I would work him over with the double of my rope. We glared at each other for a minute or two, then he tossed his head and galloped back into the fog. For the next half hour I could hear him out there, pawing and snorting, but he didn't come back into the range of my rope again.

Stanley Barby and I were always pulling pranks on each other, and I would bet that, at least for a moment, the thought crossed his mind that it would be a great prank to send me into that pasture without warning me about the stud horse. Why, it would have scared me out of six years of growth to see that phantom horse come thundering out of the fog! I was sure glad he gave me some warning, and gladder still that I was armed with my catch rope.

In the summer of 1980 Tom Ellzey and I needed to move some heifers out of the Dutcher Creek pasture. His sister Jill Ellzey was staying on the ranch that summer, so we drafted her to help with the gather. In the cool of morning we saddled up and rode a couple of miles across country. It happened that we were all riding mares that day.

When we came to the gate that opened into the Dutcher Creek pasture, Jill and I went through while Tom loped Baile, his young mare, off to the north end of the pasture. He planned to check Cottonwood Creek for tracks in the water gap to see if we might be short a few head. Jill and I rode down among the big cottonwoods that grew along the creek. It was a gorgeous summer morning, one that made you glad to be alive and ahorseback. The air was perfectly still and heavy with the fragrance of wild flowers and wild grape blooms. We decided that I would take the west side of the creek and Jill would cross over and take the east side, then we started the gather. Things went along fine for five or ten minutes before I heard a terrible racket coming from the other side of the creek: hoof beats, the squeal of horses, tree limbs snapping, and Jill yelling at the top of her lungs.

I loped toward the creek until I could see what was going on. Jill and her mare Cookie were riding around in circles, followed by a sleek sorrel horse. The sorrel was snorting, stamping his feet, and tossing his head, and Jill was turned halfway around in the saddle, trying to shoo him away. In planning our strategy, we had forgotten one small detail. The week before, we had run out of water in the Dutcher horse pasture and had turned Tuerto, the one-eyed stud, into the Dutcher Creek pasture. And here he was, in all his obnoxious stud horse glory. And we were all mounted on MARES!

Since I had tangled with stud horses before, I knew that the catch rope was the best defense. But Jill didn't carry a rope. She yelled and waved her cap in Tuerto's face, but the stud kept coming and appeared to have some notion of climbing into the saddle with her. I crossed the creek, took down my nylon, and built a loop. I galloped up behind Tuerto and whacked him three times across the behind as my little way of saying "howdy" and letting him know that playtime was over. He pulled away from Jill and Cookie and turned to face me and my mare. He gave the old stud horse squeal, shook his head, and glared at me with his gotch eye. As a colt, he'd gotten it knocked out on a tree limb. It made him look like a genuine outlaw, and also made it hard to deal with him, since he was blind on that one side.

He didn't leave, so I told Jill to go ahead with the gather and I would drive Tuerto up to the north end. I fell in behind him and spanked him with my loop, but instead of leaving, he ran around in a big circle and took aim for Cookie again. I stayed right behind him, working him over with my rope, and didn't give him a chance to molest Cookie. Then, out of sheer spite, he ran through the middle of the heifers Jill had assembled and scattered them like chickens.

I was getting mad, since I had never had much love for stud horses anyway, and for a second or two I was tempted to pitch my loop around his neck and teach him some manners. But sanity prevailed. Roping a stud off a mare didn't strike me as a very smart idea. I galloped after him and tried again to run him off. There was some bad cactus in this corner of the pasture, not the usual prickly pear but another variety that had round stems covered with long evil spines. When a horse got into it, he knew he'd been stuck with something bad.

I tried to steer Calypso around this cactus, but at last she got into it. It must have stung, because she started bucking. I put my roots down in the saddle, because I didn't have any intention of getting throwed into one of those yellow cactuses. While I was rodeoing, the stud went straight for Cookie again. Between bucks, I yelled at Jill, told her to dismount, find a stick, and fight for her life. And that's what she did. When I finally got Calypso lined out, I rode in and whipped Tuerto away, giving Jill enough time to mount up and flee for her life.

Moral: If you ride a mare, you'd better carry either a rope or a gun.

Part Two

Roping Stories

10

Unusual Targets: Wives, Kids, Dogs, Hogs, and Rabbits

$\mathcal{A}$s we have seen in the previous section, the catch rope is one of the cowboy's most important tools. It is also one of his favorite toys. Once a guy has learned to use it on cattle, he is inclined to test it out on smaller targets, just to see what might happen. Out in ranch country, many a cat and chicken has provided good wholesome entertainment for a cowboy with an idle mind and a rope in his hands.

Will Rogers probably wins the prize for roping the smallest living target. In his movie, "Roping Fool," he roped a mouse with a piece of string. And how about the largest living target? We might have to give that prize to a black cowboy in eastern New Mexico who pitched his loop on . . . let's take the yarn from the beginning. It comes from a book called *Cowboy Life on the Llano Estacado* by V. H. "Ol' Waddie" Whitlock. One day in 1906, Whitlock and several of his cowboy friends from the LFD ranch went into Roswell for some fun and entertainment.

> As we were leaving town, I saw Old Negro Ad . . . sitting on Sunflower, the most powerful roping horse in the LFD remuda. . . . We heard a commotion and, looking down the street, saw a runaway team pulling a milk wagon toward us at breakneck speed with lines flying and no driver.
>
> Ad jerked down his rope, double-half hitched one end of it to his saddle horn and built a big loop in the other end. As the team passed by, he jumped Sunflower alongside it and dropped a big "blocker" around both horses' necks. He threw the stack in his rope over the wagon, dropped his weight over in his left stirrup and turned off as if he was "fairgrounding" a big steer. Sunflower stacked the whole shebang in the middle of the street. Both horses went down, the wagon toppled on its side with the tongue broken, and milk and broken bottles scattered over a wide area. (p. 225)

The prize for roping the most elusive target must go to the Mexican ropers described by James Norman: "In northwestern Mexico, near Chihauhua, vaquero ropers were such sure shots that they captured flying Canadian geese with their singing nooses" (*Charro: Mexican Horseman*, p. 111).

Another roper of Mexican extraction, Euvence Garcia, is said to have performed an extraordinary feat with his twine. One day this King Ranch vaquero was chasing two wild colts. He caught the first one by the neck and then, holding his reins between his teeth while riding at full gallop, he took the rope off his saddle horn, built a fresh loop in the home-end, and caught the other colt with the second loop. He brought his pair of colts to a sudden stop by dropping the middle portion of the rope around a tree stump. While the colts lay on the ground, catching their breath and wondering what had happened to them, Euvence jumped off his horse and half-hitched his rope to the stump. When Euvence Garcia had a rope in his hands, according to Frank Goodwyn, "He was no longer the pitifully inadequate old creature that hobbled about the camp, but a champion to compare with the knights of King Arthur. The rope was like a live thing in his hands" (quoted in Don Hedgpeth, pp. 101-102).

Curt Brummett tells about a contest his father got into with one of those great Mexican ropers.

> My daddy was a heck of a hand with a grass rope. When he roped a horse, he'd throw a hoolihan in such a way that it would figure-eight. One part of the loop would neck the horse, and then he'd flip his rope so that the other part would halter the nose.
>
> On Saturday afternoons, when everyone else was gone, I used to wear out several herds of horses, trying to learn that loop, but I never did. (Interview, 1989)

When Brummett Sr. was a lad of seventeen and working on a ranch in Arizona, he challenged one of the Mexican cowboys to a roping contest, with a month's wages as the stakes. The Mexican— we'll call him Gomez—was known to be an expert with the rope, and he accepted the challenge. Since Brummett had issued the challenge, he made the rules. "I'm going to make three different throws and you have to make each throw just as I do. You call the horse for me and I'll call the horse for you."

Gomez agreed, and called a horse that was wise to the rope and knew all about dodging loops. Brummett's first throw was a kind of brush loop. He wadded up the loop in his right hand and threw it like a baseball at the horse. When it arrived at the target, it opened up and fell around the horse's neck.

"That's pretty good," said Gomez, "but I can do it."

Brummett went to his second throw. He laid an open loop on the ground and grasped it between two toes. "Call the horse." Gomez smiled and called the same horse. Brummett balanced himself, clasped the loop between his toes, and sent it flying at the horse. It made a catch.

"Do you want to quit now or shall I go on to the third?" he asked.

"Oh no, I can do them both. Go to the third."

"Call the horse."

Gomez called the same horse again, and the words were hardly out of his mouth before Brummett snaked out a regular hoolihan toss and fitted it around the horse's throat latch. He handed the rope to the vaquero and said, "Your turn. I call the same horse."

Gomez wadded up the rope and threw. It caught. He built a new loop, laid it on the ground, and pulled off his boot. "Same horse," said Brummett.

By this time, that old horse was getting wise to the game, but Gomez was pretty shrewd himself. He feinted with his right arm. The horse dodged, and when he did, Gomez kicked out the loop and caught him. All that remained was the simplest throw of all, and Gomez was a deadly shot with the hoolihan. Brummett called the same horse, and this time the old horse knew what was coming. The loop went flying and the horse moved and watched it fall into the dirt. Brummett put out his hand. "That'll cost you one month's wages."

Gomez was not a good loser, especially when the other cowboys were laughing at his misfortune. His face turned red. "I lose and I will pay." Then he pulled out his knife and cut the rope into pieces. "And here is your rope back!"

"That's okay, you can keep it," said Brummett. "I took it off your saddle this morning" (Interview, 1989).

A fellow I knew up in the Oklahoma Panhandle was just learning how to heel when he got married. After a short honeymoon, he and his bride moved into a little house in Beaver City and settled into a regular routine. Every evening after work, he would make his bride run around the house, while he came behind her, swinging his twine and laying in heel shots.

Another cowboy I knew used to pay his kids twenty-five cents to run around the back yard on Sunday afternoons. That worked for a while, until he miscalculated and didn't rope the little boy deep enough. He put a rope burn on the lad's cheek and mama passed a law against roping her children.

I used to work on a ranch that was blessed with a couple of so-called cowdogs. They were typical of ranch curs in this part of the country: loyal, friendly, and utterly worthless. They had about as much cow-sense as a Stilson wrench, but there was one part of cowboy work they picked up real quick. They knew about that rope. When you had a rope in your hands, you couldn't get those dogs to trot along in front of a horse. I tried it many times. Old Drover would be loafing along beside me and I would reach for my twine. Suddenly Drover would disappear, and later I would see him, a safe fifteen feet behind me. The only way I ever caught that dog was with a hoolihan, thrown blind and backward in one quick sweep. It was a lucky shot, and I only did it once. This was the same dog, by the way, who served as the model for Drover in my Hank the Cowdog books.

I didn't have much luck roping dogs, and I can't say that it made me any wiser or richer. But in a little book called *Pecos Tales II* Paul Patterson tells of a West Texas cowboy who actually *made money* roping dogs. Young Lee was one of those legendary old-time ropers who was revered by the small circle of ranch cowboys who had seen him in action, yet unknown to most of the world. It was said that he could work a branding herd all day long and keep three sets of flankers running, heeling one calf after another without ever missing a throw.

He came from the big ranch country around Midland, Texas, the same country that produced such legendary figures as Foy and Leonard Proctor, Buster Welch, and J. Evetts Haley. After a long and colorful career as a cowboy, Lee retired and moved into town, "to while away his remaining years in the Scharbauer Hotel lobby," swapping stories with other cowboys. But Midland was having a problem with stray dogs, and someone came up with the idea of hiring Young Lee to rope them. The city "rigged up a wagon with a high net-wire cage, put a driver on the seat and a couple of bouncers in the back," and Young Lee rode alongside on a little brown pony.

When a dog came near, "suddenly, a strange snake-like something whistled out of nowhere, snatched a pooch and swung him to a bouncer in the wagon. . . . In what seemed like one deft stroke, Young Lee would snare a mutt, swing it up, have a new loop shook out and another dog nabbed before poor Bowser's expression could switch from wonder to horror." Paul Patterson says that while dog-roping lacked the prestige of fairgrounding steers, "the pay was better than cow-punching. Young Lee was getting paid by the dog instead of by the day" (pp. 10-12).

In the December 1959 issue of *Western Horseman*, Bill Leftwich wrote about a Mexican roper named Conrado Gomez who made his living roping pigs for the State of Guanajuato Foot-and-Mouth Commission.

> Roping hogs is so different from roping cattle that a new set of throws must be learned. In roping cattle, the loop is thrown so that it will settle horizontally over the horns or head; in pig roping, the target is much smaller and without horns! To catch pigs, the loop must stand up vertically like a hoop. . . ." (pp. 48-49)

Leftwich says that Gomez used a hard twist maguey rope that was ideal for this type of roping—which required some spring in the rope—and that Gomez would rope all day long and miss no more than two or three loops.

But my favorite story about unusual roping targets is one told by my good friend Frankie McWhorter of the Gray Ranch in Lipscomb County, Texas. The night he told me this story in his kitchen, I thought he was making it up, but he swore that it was true. Here it is, in Frankie's own words.

> In 1957 I was in Memphis, Texas, breaking horses on my own. After a while I began to notice that most of my business was coming from Childress, Texas, so I moved down there and went to work.
>
> I was keeping my horses out at the sale barn and helping them at the sale every Wednesday. I'd push

cattle to them on sale day and they'd pay me more than I was making breaking horses, the reason being that nobody paid me.

I was riding them horses and day-working some besides that. When I got one doing well enough, I'd take him and go help someone gather cattle, and while I was gone, people would come and pick up their horses.

Well, an old boy down there approached me with the idea of putting on a jackrabbit roping contest. We were all going to get rich on the deal. He said, "We'll cut you in on the profits." I thought that sounded like a winner. *Anybody* would come to a jackrabbit roping, just to see what it was.

So we put it on the radio, had posters made, did some publicity.

The way we got these rabbits, we cut the bead out of a tractor tire and wove some fishing cord across it and made a kind of a net thing. It took five men to catch those jackrabbits. We'd go out at night to that old air base at Childress and there was a world of rabbits out there 'cause they'd sowed it to wheat.

We had a spotlight and a man standing up in the back of the pickup with a .22. If the rabbit ran, he'd shoot in front of him a foot or so and turn him back. Then he'd shoot in front of him again. If he ran straight away, he shot over the top of him and he'd stop. Then we'd drive up and pitch that net on him and we'd have to jump off and get on it or he'd run off with it.

That's the way we got 'em, and we had *seventy-three* of them things in my basement. Lord God . . . stink! The maddest wife! I was taking alfalfa hay down there to 'em and she was having to water 'em, and mad! Uncommonly mad.

They were running loose in that basement and when you walked down there, quite a bit happened.

Two or three of them had babies and they'd jump on you when you went down there. Don't think them mama rabbits won't jump on you and whack you with their hind feet.

We took a strand of chicken wire, that little chicken wire, and put it around the inside of the roping arena, and in the catch pen we had little boxes covered with gunny sacks. We ran those rabbits the day before the roping. We turned them aloose in the calf chute and busted their butts and made 'em run. When they found out there was a sanctuary on the other end, they'd go to it.

We ran 'em twice, and boy, that second time they made a bee line for that other end.

I don't remember how many ropers we had, but each one got two head of rabbits. A lot of them was local. Those old boys would nod for their rabbit and them old horses would come out of there hunting for a calf. The rabbit would stop and the horse would go on.

But there was one boy, I'd known him since he was little, his name was Clifton Smith. His daddy was Will T. Smith from Tell, Texas, and he was a calf roper. Clifton later won the Cheyenne Frontier Days calf roping.

Will was smarter than the rest. He'd watched those other boys going after their rabbits. Nobody caught one and he figured out a plan.

He'd brought a little rope, wasn't as big around as a cigarette, and he didn't chase his rabbit. He just kind of headed it off. He didn't run out there and try to rope it like the others had done, 'cause you can't drag your slack on a jackrabbit.

He cut that rabbit off, and when it hit the fence and sat up, Clifton whapped a hoolihan on that general, got down, and brought him to us. And that's the only one that was caught out of them seventy-three rabbits. Clifton won all the money, all three places.

After the roping, we had to dispose of the rabbits. There were some greyhound people out there and we sold them the rabbits for six bits apiece. And when we paid the promotional expenses and took the price of the chicken wire off, I think I made $3.75 and lost two weeks' sleep. (McWhorter and Erickson, *Cowboy Fiddler*, 70-72)

Frankie McWhorter and his horse Sunday in 1992, bringing a calf to the fire at the Bussard Ranch branding in Lipscomb County, Texas. After making his fortune in the jackrabbit business, Frankie filled his idle hours working as a cowboy, ranch foreman, horse breaker, and fiddler in the northern Panhandle. *Courtesy of photographer, Kris Erickson.*

11
Things That Ort Not to Be Roped

Roping skill, like any other skill, comes hard. To rope well, a man must put in hours, days, years of practice. While the rest of the human race is busy doing sensible things that will bring fame or fortune, the cowboy is out playing with his twine, throwing at anything that even remotely resembles a target: sagebrush, soapweed, fence posts, cinder blocks, and trash cans. After he has roped inanimate objects long enough to perfect his throw and handle his coils, he begins to tire of targets that don't move. He starts looking around for live meat. He knows that gratuitious roping of ranch stock can get a man into trouble, so he must find other targets: mice, geese, cats, chickens, wives, kids, dogs, hogs, and rabbits. Roping little stuff, he can't get himself into much trouble, but sometimes he goes on to bigger stock and starts putting his twine on things that ort not to be roped. There, he finds out how much trouble a rope can cause.

In his book, *A Texas Cow Boy*, Charlie Siringo tells about the time he decided he ought to rope a yearling heifer—a *buffalo* heifer, that is.

When the rope tightened the yearling began to bleat and its mammy broke back out of the herd and took after me. I tried to turn the rope loose so as to get out of the way, but couldn't, as it was drawn very tight around the saddle horn.

Ma Buffalo worked Charlie's pony over for a while, then ran back to the herd. That left him with only one problem. Once you have caught a yearling buffalo, how do you get your rope back?

That's the kind of question a cowboy ought to ask *before* he makes his toss, but somehow it rarely works out that way. Siringo threw trips on the heifer, trying to break her neck or at least to bed her down, but every time he threw her, she bounced back up. He tried to cut his rope but his pocketknife was too dull to cut. At last the matter came down to hand-to-hand combat. Charlie dismounted, walked down the rope, and fought the buffalo until she was more exhausted than he was: "It was pitch dark when I started towards camp," he relates, "with the hide and a small chunk of meat tied behind my saddle" (pp. 151-53). It is worth noting that there is no mention in the book of Siringo trying this stunt a second time.

In J. Frank Dobie's *A Vaquero of the Brush Country*, John Young tells of his introduction into elk roping in Colorado.

I let my horse run along ahead of the elk, and then as a big stag passed me with a snort I twined him about one horn and half a head. He was bounding along with great leaps and at the instant he reached the end of the rope [he] was in midair. The jerk whirled him around and he hit the ground flat. He bounced to his feet like a rubber ball and ran on the rope again, but this time I did not throw him.

I could see that he was getting mad. He quit running; his hair stood straight up; he looked at me viciously for a few seconds; then he shook his head and came straight for me.

John Young, like Charlie Siringo, began to regret what he had done and started thinking about his pocketknife. But Young had an able cowboy partner with him that day, and at the last moment his friend dashed in and double-hocked the beast and laid him down. Then all they had to do was get their ropes back, get ahorseback, and flee for their lives, for the elk "had blood in his eye, and right there we had to do some tall riding" (pp. 179-80).

In the same book, John Young claims to have roped an antelope, a buffalo calf, and a bobcat, "the out-fightingest animal that I ever roped" (p. 258). Then he gives this sound advice to young ropers:

> If a man ropes a buck deer or a black bear, he had
> better keep his rope tight and drag the animal down
> or else prepare either to shoot or to cut loose. If given
> a chance, a bear will climb down a rope, and a buck
> deer will try to gore both man and horse. (p. 257)

In Barney Nelson's *The Last Campfire*, old-time rancher Ted Gray tells about roping deer in the Davis Mountains of West Texas:

> For a change of pace, and when the chance arose, the
> cowboys sometimes roped a deer for camp meat. Once
> Nick came barreling off a hill about two and a half
> miles from camp, right behind a big buck. He ran him
> right up to the wagon, roped him, and Ted ran out to
> meet him with the ax. Nick then proceeded to butcher
> his deer on the spot. (p. 64)

John Young relates the story about an Arizona cowboy who ran across one of the camels Jefferson Davis brought to the American Southwest while he was Secretary of War. The camel had escaped and gone wild, and the Arizona cowboy couldn't pass up a chance to rope it, just to see what would happen. He made his catch, but the camel broke his cinches and ran off with a $50 saddle (Dobie, *Vaquero*, p. 255).

In *The Longhorns*, J. Frank Dobie tells about a South Texas cowboy named Jacinto de los Santos who was helping John Blocker catch wild cattle in the brush before daylight. In the gloom, Jacinto saw what he thought was a calf up ahead. He tossed out a little loop and made the catch. "The thing would not stay down," he told Dobie later. "Never in all my life did I feel such another animal on the end of the rope. It could bounce like a rubber ball." He began to think that

COW POKES   By Ace Reid

"It's your rope, you go get it!"

Courtesy of Ace Reid Enterprises, Kerrville, Texas.

he had caught the Devil himself, but when daylight came, he found that he was tied to a panther (pp. 312-14).

I knew a fellow up on the Beaver River who couldn't resist smearing his new braided nylon on a full-grown badger. He figured he would have his fun, drag the badger to death, and then get back to the roundup work. Badgers, he soon discovered, don't drag to death, and neither do they have much of a sense of humor. By the time this cowboy was ready to coil up his rope and move along, the badger was tuned up for a fight. He climbed the rope and tried to climb the horse, and the cowboy had to drag him in a circle for fifteen minutes, until another man arrived to help him.

Charlie Russell did a painting in 1904 called "Roping a Wolf," which shows three northern cowboys out on a lark. One of them has roped a wolf, and his pals are coming up behind him with their loops in the air. In *Trails Plowed Under* he relates the story of a cowboy named Bill Bullard who ran into a couple of wolves. He roped the first one, dallied the middle of his rope around the horn, built a new loop on the home-end, and caught the second wolf. When the wolves started snapping at his horse, the old pony broke in half and bucked all the way back to camp. Bill Bullard's comment on this lark was, "Maybe you'll kill two birds with one stone but don't ever bet you can get two anythings with one rope" (pp. 23-24). Arnold Rojas recalled that vaqueros on the Miller and Lux ranch in California used to rope coyotes, brand them with the S Wrench, bob their tails, and put the Miller ear mark on them (p. 40).

Charlie Russell did paintings of cowboys roping bears, and in *Cowboy Culture*, David Dary tells about California vaqueros roping bears in the nineteenth century:

> When vaqueros tired of braiding horsehair ropes or of catching horses and cattle and even elk and deer, they would seek out grizzly bears to have some fun. . . . On a grizzly hunt one night in the early 1830s, Don Jose Joaquin Estudillo and ten soldiers, who had been va-queros, lassoed and killed forty bears in the woods. . . . (pp. 65-66)

Dary says the bears were roped by the neck and hind legs and strangled when the horses pulled in opposite directions.

California vaqueros were not the only ones who engaged in bear-roping. In *Charles Goodnight: Cowman and Plainsman*, J. Evetts Haley tells about the time when Frank Mitchell, one of Colonel Goodnight's JA cowboys, stuck his loop on a half-grown black bear. He dragged the bear back to headquarters where another man roped its heels and another brought out a hot iron and branded the JA on the bear's hip. When they turned him loose, the bear ran to the mess hall and kitchen, where a Mrs. Devier was washing the breakfast dishes with her baby nearby.

> When the bear broke into the door, she grabbed the child, and in panic pitched it out the window, fainted, and fell into the woodbox behind the stove. Old Bruin passed into the mess-hall, jumped up on the long table, and went out through the window at the end of the room, carrying the sash with him. . . . He came near breaking up the ranch, and anybody else would have been fired for causing such a commotion, but Mitchell escaped with a good rimmin' out. (p. 408)

Mr. Haley notes that "as long as Texas cowboys have been tying their ropes hard and fast to their saddle horns, they have been roping any and everything that wore hair, and a good many things that don't" (p. 406).

In my book *Through Time and the Valley*, I tell about a girl named Sena Walstad who lived on a ranch near the Canadian River in the Texas Panhandle:

> One summer day in 1887, while riding up Picket Canyon, she saw a half-grown bear lumbering through the brush ahead of her. Most girls—and boys too—would have left the scene in a hurry, but not Sena Walstad. Calmly she took the rope from her saddle,

> coaxed her frightened horse into range, roped the bear, dragged it home, and made a pet of it. (p. 56)

By the way, in 1991 I bought that ranch where Sena Walstad roped the bear back in 1887, and I now write my books in Picket Canyon, where we have a log home. I haven't seen any black bears in the canyon, but if I ever do see one, I solemnly swear not to put a loop on it.

In a *Western Horseman* article, Phil Livingston gives an account of a hair-raising South Texas sport, hunting wild hogs on horseback.

> These rooters are the descendants of razorbacks that got loose from the early settlers a couple of hundred years ago. . . . An old boar of this strain can weigh 400 pounds, is fast and agile on his feet, isn't afraid of anything, and will have sharp tusks up to 6 inches long. . . . (pp. 40-44)

Following their dogs through the dense brush, the horsemen wait for the hog to break into a clearing so they can get a shot with their ropes. If they don't, the beast will brush up and the hunters go in on foot and grab a hind leg while the hog is fighting the hounds.

High on my list of things that ort not to be roped and loops that should never be thrown is one used by Mexican vaqueros in their *charreadas*, or roping contests. The throw is called *paso de la muerte* ("throw of death"), and James Norman describes it *Charro: Mexican Horseman*:

> To execute this exciting throw the roper works on foot. He firmly ties his two legs together with several loops of the home end of his lariat and secures it with a slip knot. With the remainder of the rope loosely coiled in his left hand and whirling the throwing loop with his right hand, he throws a *mangana*, lassoing the hind legs of a running wild mare. As the rope is played out, the man's legs are jerked out from be-

neath him, and he is dragged by the horse. When the
horse finally halts, the man pulls the slipknot and stands
up. (p. 115)

I have ridden with some crazy cowboys, but I never knew one who
was crazy enough to try that one.

Speaking of crazy cowboys, Curt Brummett of Maljamar, New
Mexico, describes himself as a fellow who grew up with a rope in his
hands and would rope anything his horse could catch. "I always wanted
to rope a kangaroo but I never quite made it to Australia," he says.
When he was a boy growing up on ranches in Eastern New Mexico,
he always carried the broken and cast-off ropes of the older men. But
then one day his daddy went to the coil of silk manila and cut him off
a new rope of his very own. After tying a honda in the home-end, he
presented it to young Curt with this piece of advice: "Don't ever put
it on anything that won't give it back in one piece."

Not long after this, Curt was sitting around the cook shack with
his dad and the other cowboys. Curt's mother brewed a big pot of
coffee, put it on a tray with cups, and walked into the room. "I had
that rope in my hands," he remembered, "and why I decided to forefoot my mother, I don't know, but I did. Just flipped a loop out there
and caught her." She tripped on the rope and dumped the hot coffee
into Mr. Brummett's lap. Cowboys scattered. Mrs. Brummett picked
herself up off the floor and headed for Curt.

"Give me that rope!" she said. He did, expecting to be thrashed
with it. Instead, she did something far worse—marched into the kitchen,
pulled out a butcher knife, and proceeded to cut Curt's new rope into
a dozen pieces. Father Brummett watched this with a smirk. "I told
you not to put that rope on anything that wouldn't give it back in one
piece" (interview 1989).

In the lore and literature of the West, there are plenty of stories
about cowboys who roped things that ort not to be roped. Yet I'm
sure it goes on today, just as it did 100 years ago. As Philip Ashton
Rollins observed in 1922, "The West would lariat anything that suddenly bobbed up in front and looked saucy" (p. 184).

12
The Blocker Loop
in Mississippi

Toward the end of September 1984, I was in eastern Mississippi for a Braford field day. This was pulpwood and lumber country, yet I found something over there that I hadn't expected: a group of young fellers who were as rope-crazy as any Texas cowboys I'd ever met, including me. As near as I could gather, most of them were raised up on small farms that ran a few half-bramer cattle in the woods. There weren't many good horses around and the cattle were cowboyed with a pickup, a feed sack, and dogs. They worked a lot of dogs down there, but not many people used a rope. Those who did tied hard-and-fast—or as they call it in Mississippi, "hard-and-tight."

When these guys came of age, most of them didn't have the option of staying in agriculture. The land holdings were too small and the money just wasn't there, so they took jobs. David went into the pulpwood business. Mike worked in the oil field. Donald became a welder, Roy a cattle inspector for the state. Randy and Larry had enough country to put together a registered Braford business, with timber on the side.

I don't know how they got started roping. Maybe Randy and Larry brought in some good horses to use on their place. Then someone went to a roping school and came back with the fever. It spread fast. Before long, they had a little roping club. Each member kicked in $25 annual dues and one roping steer. They learned how to dally and handle cattle on a loose rope. They went to Kansas and Texas to buy horses with proven blood-lines and took them to jackpot ropings in the next county. Then they built an arena out at Randy and Larry's place. And they put up *lights*, an indication that the lads were serious about this. Where you find lights, you find cowboys roping long into the night.

Roping became their passion and the focus of their social life. Every weekend, they took their families with them to the arena. Maybe the women weren't as excited about spending long hours at the arena as the men were, but surely they knew what other cowboy wives have come to realize—that a man could have worse habits than roping, and could spend his time in worse places than an arena. Once they had learned to catch in the arena, it was inevitable that they would move outside. Once you have a skill, you want to use it. Once you've solved the problems posed by an arena, you begin to wonder how well you would do under pasture conditions.

It started one day when some of the ropers were in a cafe and overheard some local farmers talking about outlawed stock that "couldn't be gathered." It was hard to tell if the farmers were complaining or bragging. Each tried to match the others' stories about wild cattle. The ropers decided to take the challenge. They moved over to the farmers' table and said, "I bet we can gather your cattle." The farmers looked them over and grinned. "Not much chance of that, boys. We've tried everything—feed, dogs, pickups, traps. Nothing works."

"Give us a chance. If we can't handle it, we won't charge you a dime."

"How do you figger on gathering 'em?"

"We'll use dogs and horses and ropes."

"Ropes? You mean you'll rope the cattle?"

"That's right."

The farmers wagged their heads and sipped their coffee. "Rope's too hard on cattle."

This was not big ranch country and it had no roping tradition. These small farmer-stockmen had never used a rope and they were suspicious of anyone who could. You can understand why stockmen in Mississippi might be suspicious of the rope, but the odd thing is that I've heard exactly the same words from ranchers in Texas and Oklahoma. It seems that, with only a few exceptions, cattlemen all over the country abandoned roping as a legitimate ranch technique sometime in the 1940s, or maybe even earlier. They went to pens and squeeze chutes because it was easier, because it required less manpower, because it didn't take any practice or skill to run a chute.

That generation of cattlemen has a hard time understanding the new breed of ropers, who have spent uncounted hours throwing at a roping dummy and gone to the arena to learn skills that "everyone" has decided are out of date. Why would a guy spend his hard-earned money on a horse and saddle, a pickup, a trailer, a stack of ropes, and a bunch of roping steers? And why would he volunteer to go out into the dark pine forest and do battle with the meanest, rankest, fightingest stock in the county? It's hard to explain. It goes against common sense and economic reality. To understand those ropers in Mississippi, maybe you need to have some cowboy in you. Cowboying has always been an assault on common sense. There never was any money in it, even in the good years, and the ratio of hours-to-dollars, multiplied by broken bones, has made it something close to folly.

Those young guys in the cafe wanted to go after rank stock. They were pumpers and welders by trade, but they wanted to get a taste of cowboying—not squeeze-chute cowboying, but the kind that demands skill, horseflesh, and guts. Well, the farmers weren't going to have any of that rope business on their places. "We'll just wait and get 'em in with a feed sack." But a few weeks later, one of the farmers had thought it over and decided to give the ropers a chance. He had a fighting bull out in the timber and he told the ropers to gather him up. Or at least to try.

The ropers didn't intend to *try*. They intended to do the job. They rode into the pines with horses and dogs. The dogs found the bull and "bayed him up." When he broke and ran, the cowboys went after him, and when he hit a little clearing, the man on the fastest horse put a rope on him. To get the bull out, they had to put a second rope on him and pull him with two horses. When the horses wore down, they tied the bull to a tree, rested the horses, and then pulled some more, until they reached a spot where they could get in with a pickup and trailer.

They delivered the bull, and the word began to spread that there were some wild cow catchers in the area. They began getting calls from other farmers who had wild stock. By the time they got a job, it was a case of last resort. The owner had already exhausted all reasonable methods and the animal had established himself as a genuine outlaw.

One of these calls sent them to a small town in the south part of Clarke County. A wild cow had gone through several fences, swum a river, and ended up in the city limits. She was one of those half-bramer cows with a big set of horns, and she was sure in a nasty frame of mind. The cowboys went after her on horses and with dogs, down Main Street and across the railroad tracks. She ducked into a lumber mill and sent the hired hands scattering onto trucks and stacks of lumber. At last the dogs got her cornered and the horsemen rode in and put several ropes around her horns. They loaded her into a trailer and delivered her to the owner. They were paid $65, which they had to give to the owner of the lumber mill to pay for a cyclone fence the cow had destroyed.

At the time I met these guys, they'd only come up with one job they couldn't handle. They'd been sent out to catch a 1900-pound

COW POKES   **By Ace Reid**

"Stand still Jake, or she's gonna think yore scared!"

Courtesy of Ace Reid Enterprises, Kerrville, Texas.

crossbred bull that was running in a pine and saw-briar forest—about
the worst roping conditions you could imagine. Since a horse couldn't
travel through most of this country, they turned out their dogs. When
the dogs bayed the bull, the cowboys followed the sound and set up
in a small clearing. When the bull hit the clearing, they built to him,
and the first man there had time for one quick throw.

They got him caught, but he came back up the rope, got under
the horse, and knocked him down. In the process, he slipped out of
the rope and escaped. These Mississippi cowboys weren't easily
spooked, but they weren't anxious to put another head loop on 1900
pounds of pure meanness. They went to town and borrowed a tran-

quilizer gun from a vet, returned to the woods and shot the bull with two tranquilizer darts.

It didn't faze him, and he was still running loose at the time I heard the story. But my cowboys friends were plotting their revenge. On Saturday evening, after the field day and barbecue, several of us gravitated around a roping dummy. These boys only knew two loops, the regular head and heel shots used in team roping, but they had them down cold. Roy, David, and Larry could stand in front of the dummy and throw a hundred times without a miss.

I showed them several old-time loops I'd picked up from cowboys in Texas and Oklahoma, including the hoolihan and the Blocker, loops known to Charlie Russell, Charles Goodnight, and Ben K. Green. I was especially proud of the Blocker because it had taken me years to find someone who could show me how to throw it. Those boys in Mississippi were hungry to learn anything new about roping, and they picked up the Blocker right away. By midnight, after we had spent four solid hours on the roping dummy, they were throwing the Blocker as well as I could.

Later, driving to the motel, it occurred to me why they had been so anxious to learn the Blocker. I had learned it just for fun and had never used it in the pasture. But those boys intended to use it the very next week—on that waspy 1900-pound bull out in the woods. You could say about these fellows, "Well, they're not ranch cowboys. They're only playing around." True, but in the process of "playing around" they had not only become excellent arena ropers, but they were going out and doing the sort of things that Ben Green wrote about in *Wild Cow Tales*—and had every intention of using that old forgotten Blocker loop that Ben Green had used every day.

There is a post script to this story. In January 1985, one of the Mississippi boys called to tell me that they had used the Blocker on the old bull, had caught him and managed to get him out of the woods and to a sale barn. But the rascal was so wild and so mad about being caught that he refused to eat or drink. He just laid down and died.

13

The Pasture Roping Contest

I t was going to be an epic battle: ranch cowboys versus arena ropers, in a contest that would place them on equal footing. This was to be a roping contest held under pasture conditions, in a two-section pasture on the Charles Ware LS Ranch west of Amarillo. I had just sold an article or two and happened to have $150 for the entry fee. I signed me and Tom Ellzey up as a team, and then I asked Tom if he wanted to enter. The thought of entering a roping contest scared him almost as badly as it scared me. That's why I had sent the money in first. That way we couldn't back out.

Tom and I considered ourselves pretty salty pasture ropers. Team roping in the pasture was one of our regular jobs, and in typical cowboy fashion, we were as vain about our roping skills as a couple of roosters. Yet roping in competition, in front of a crowd, was something we had never done before. We were nervous about it but also excited. We knew the arena boys were unbeatable in the arena. But out in the pasture . . . that was *our* game. We might not win the pot, but we figured we could show the arena boys how roping was done out in the real West.

The arena boys had speed, hot rod horses, and the advantage of constant practice. But they were accustomed to working in an artificial environment where the footing was good and the cattle ran straight. It seemed reasonable to assume that neither the men nor the horses would be able to make the adjustment from arena to pasture, and for that reason, I felt the working cowboys would have a slight advantage.

Before daylight on June 15, 1980, we saddled Happy and Calypso, loaded them in the ranch trailer, and began the three-hour drive to the Ware Ranch. West of Amarillo, the country changed from the plains and rolling buffalo grass hills we were accustomed to. We saw red soil and broken country covered with mesquite brush and cholla cactus. We wondered what our horses would think about that cactus, which stood as tall as a tree and was covered with wicked spines. They had never seen cholla before.

We pulled off the highway and drove toward a swarm of pickups and trailers parked out in the pasture. Some of the pickups bore the names of ranches in the area: LS, Coldwater Cattle Company, Weymouth Ranch, and others. At the center of the gathering was a platform for the secretary, announcer, and the timekeepers. Beside it were thirty-two horned, cat-hammed corriente steers that weighed around 500 pounds each. They were as lean as greyhounds and looked as though they could run all the way back to Mexico without stopping. Just to the south of the judges' platform was a refreshment tent, shading a dozen folding chairs and two stock tanks filled with ice and cold beverages—Big Red and RC Cola in one, Coors and Millers in the other. No water. It appeared that most of the ropers were visiting the beer tank, and some of them had been visiting it since the crack of dawn. The day had turned off hot and windy, and while Tom and I were tempted to have a cold one or two, we didn't dare. This was serious business.

During the Calcutta, we unloaded our horses and rode out the country east of the holding pen where the cattle would be running. The first 200 yards in front of the chute was fairly open and level ground, broken only by a couple of deep cow paths and a small amount of mesquite. If a man could get his steer caught quickly, he

This team at the ranch roping got their steer caught just in time, before he dived into the mesquite. Tom and the author weren't so lucky. *Courtesy of photographer, Kris Erickson.*

would do all right. But the farther east we went, the heavier the brush became—big mesquites and those wicked cholla cactuses. The ground was still fairly level, but that brush would cause problems. We could hear the Calcutta over the P.A. system, as the crowd bid on teams they thought might win. Our names came up and nobody bid. I guess we didn't look very impressive.

At noon the announcer called the ropers to the box. We were the twelfth team out of sixty-five. Most of the ropers rode big, leggy part-thoroughbred horses that had been selected for speed. Digger Howard of Amarillo had furnished the stock for the event, and these corrientes had never been roped before. On the first go-round they didn't know exactly what to do. They walked or trotted out into the 100-foot neutral zone, sniffed the ground, and looked at the scenery. Many had to be hazed across the chalk score line.

One of the steers in the first go-round put on quite a show. After crossing the score line, he turned south and headed toward the refreshment tent, with two cowboys thundering right behind him. The header chased him through the parking area, scattering spectators and evoking yells and laughter from the ropers on the other side. The steer ran back to the holding pen—hoping to get back in, I think—then made a dash for some pickups and trailers to the north. The header spurred hard and stuck a loop on him just as he reached the parking area. He dallied and turned off, swinging the steer in a big circle. While the crowd laughed and yelled, "Western! Western!" the steer slammed into the side of a red Dodge pickup with New Mexico tags, knocking off a chrome strip and leaving a dent in the door. As soon as the steer bounced off the pickup, the heeler moved in and picked up double-hocks. And there, in the middle of the parking lot, they bedded him down. The time wasn't so good, but by George, they had caught their cow.

No, it wasn't going to be an ordinary roping contest.

The steers didn't run hard on the first go and there were very few missed loops. I got our steer caught before he reached the bad brush. Calypso gave me the position I wanted, I pitched the loop on him, and got him turned. Tom missed his first heel loop but came up with one hock on his second. We hadn't set the world on fire but we hadn't done too badly either. At least we were still in the game.

By the time we went out with our second steer, those corrientes had figured out the game: run like crazy and hit the brush. And they did. It took a pretty good horse just to stay up with them. The boys who had come with racehorses stayed in the money. Those of us riding common old ranch horses never had a chance. Calypso was a good pasture horse. She could do a little bit of everything and put in a hard day's work. But she had never had great speed, even though her mama had run on the track for a while, and she had never seen cattle run like those corrientes.

Looking back, I think we made a mistake putting me and Calypso on the head. Happy was the better sprinter of the two, and Tom was better at throwing long than I. We had put me on the heads because, given good position, I was more accurate than Tom, while he usually did better on the heels than I. But after the first go-round, I never got good position or anything close to it.

My second steer shot out of the box like a jackrabbit. I couldn't have hit him with a .30-.06, let alone with a head loop. He flew across the open country and hit the brush. I whipped and spurred and followed him. My little mare had been trained to follow cattle, and that's just what she did—right into the middle of the mesquite and cholla. We plowed on. I dodged a mesquite limb as big around as my leg, lost both stirrups, and heard Tom behind me, yelling, "Git 'im, John!" That was a nice idea. We came to a clearing about the size of an average bathroom and I threw long. Thank God I missed. I don't know what I would have done with the steer if I'd caught him, since I was about two-thirds out of the saddle and had nearly lost my shirt to that last mesquite.

We let him go, but vowed that on our third and final steer we would rope fast and aim for the go-round money. On the third go, we drew another greyhound who made a mockery of our strategy to rope fast. I needed a road map just to find the son of a gun. He hit the brush and we went in behind him. I was mad by then, determined to catch him even if I had to run him all the way to Dumas. It was about that time that one of those eight-foot cholla cactuses loomed up in front of us. Calypso couldn't decide whether to pass it on the left or right, so she split the difference and ran through the middle of it. We emerged wearing all the cactus we hadn't knocked to the ground. It began with a six-inch chunk on Calypso's left jaw and left a clear trail down her neck and shoulder and across my leg. Tom and Happy leveled the one that we missed.

Well, that was about all the pasture roping I needed for one day. I threw my rope, just for appearances, and we headed back to the beer tank. We had been outrun, outsmarted, outdodged, and outbrushed, and we were a couple of humble cowboys when we crawled out of the brush. Tom got a pair of fencing pliers out of his pickup, and we spent the next hour pulling cholla spines out of our horses and ourselves. For the next month Tom and I had red dots that started at our boot tops and ran all the way up to our hips. Cactus tracks and memories were all we got for our $150.

We weren't the only team that washed out in the third go-round. A lot of them did. But the surprising thing to me was that the contest went all the way to the fifth go with seven or eight teams still in contention. The winning team, John Walden and John Wilson of Hereford, won the average with a time of 26.7 seconds per run. That wouldn't win you a sack of popcorn in the arena, but under the conditions of this contest it wasn't bad at all.

Who won the contest, the ranch cowboys or the arena ropers? I made some inquiries about the top five teams, and the pattern I found was that while most of the top ropers had some ranch or feedlot work in their background, none was a working ranch cowboy, and all were active arena ropers. The ranch cowboys got blown away, is what it amounted to, and the arena ropers proved that their skills could transfer from arena to pasture. On that particular day and in that particular pasture, the arena boys were clearly better than we were.

Tom and I had a terrible time accepting this, and for the next two months we talked of how we might have set up the course so that we might have come out looking better. We figured that if the course had been run in rougher country, with rocks and ravines, canyons and hills, our ranch-bred horses would have done better. A rougher course would have slowed down those racehorses and given our mounts a chance to use their sure feet and pasture savvy.

Yes, the death loss on cowboys and horses would have been high in such a contest, but that was a small price to pay for a prize buckle for me and Tom. But the simple fact was that we had been beaten at our own game. No matter how hard you try, you simply can't deny the skill of today's arena ropers. They are, quite simply, the best and fastest headers and heelers ever to walk the earth. They are better than the arena ropers of fifty years ago, and they are better than the ranch cowboys of today.

If you're a working cowboy, vain about your roping ability, it sure hurts to admit this. But, after all, most of what we ranch cowboys know about roping came from those boys in the arena. They pioneered and mastered the techniques of modern roping, and whether we like it or not, the teachers are still better than the students.

But if Tom and I ever host a pasture roping contest, we'll figure out a way to win a buckle.

14

The Swimming Heifer

One day in July, 1979, I was checking the cattle on summer pastures and found that I was one heifer short on the Smith place, west of Knowles, Oklahoma. Paul and Fred Barby had a herd of cows and calves in the pasture that joined us on the west, and I figured the heifer had gone visiting across the fence.

I had Calypso with me that day. She was a young green colt at that time but I was starting to ease her into my string of using horses. I drove the pickup and trailer over to Paul and Fred's pasture, unloaded Calypso, and rode through the cattle. I found the heifer and tried to drive her back to her home pasture. I couldn't split her away from the cows, so I roped her and drove her to the trailer. I eased her up to the back end, flipped my rope over the racks, and started pulling her in.

This should have been a simple job, because the heifer only weighed 500 pounds, and if I had been mounted on a stouter horse, it would have been easy. But Calypso was small and still green, and she hadn't learned how to pull a heavy load. The heifer sulled at the mouth of the trailer, and when I spurred Calypso hard, she started bucking. I was dallied, but the rope pinned my arm so that I couldn't release my wraps around the horn. For a moment or two, things got tense, with Calypso bucking and winding me up in the rope. At last I was able to release my dally and ride out of it. The heifer ran off with my rope and I spent half an hour getting it back. I loaded the heifer in the trailer and took her back to the pasture.And then I took Miss Calypso down to the Beaver River and we spent the rest of the afternoon dragging logs through the sand, until she figured out what she was supposed to do with a load—pull it.

A week later I checked the heifers on the Smith place and once again I came up short on my count. The same heifer had strayed again, and I figured I would find her with Paul and Fred's cows. This was a rough little pasture. Unlike most of the country north of the Beaver River, it had no sandhills, but was composed of tight soil which tended to wash into deep ditches and ravines. To help control the problem of soil erosion, Paul and Fred had built a dam across the main draw in the pasture.

We'd had big rains that spring, and a pond of about ten acres had collected behind the dam. In that dry country, it was a big lake. I rode past the lake and checked a bunch of cows in the northeast corner of the pasture. The heifer was with them. I didn't even try to cut her away from the cows this time, but just went ahead and roped her. I dallied up and brought her to a stop to let her know that she was caught and would be taking orders from me and Calypso. Then I got behind her, slacked the rope, and started driving her toward the trailer.

If you're a dally man, you drive a captured animal with a loose rope—that is, you unwrap the dally from the horn. That way you can control the slack so that if the animal happens to stop or slow down, your horse won't step over the rope with her front feet. You control the slack by holding the rope up above your head and letting out or taking up the coils in your left hand. If the animal gets too far ahead of you and takes out too much rope, you can always dally.

I drove the heifer south toward the trailer. We were moving along just fine when all at once she broke into a run down a long hill

COW POKES

By Ace Reid

"Lessee, if I turn loose the rope to grab the horn
I'll loose my calf and rope, and if I don't, I'll
loose my reputation as a great bronc rider!"

Courtesy of Ace Reid Enterprises, Kerrville, Texas.

toward the lake. I still held a loose rope, so I had to spur Calypso into
a run to keep up with her. The heifer was moving in the right direction and I didn't care whether she ran or walked, as long as I didn't
fall too far behind and get the rope jerked out of my hand before I
could take a wrap. But the farther down the hill we went, the faster

the heifer ran. Calypso was jumping ditches and cow trails now, and I began to feel uneasy about this. We were going too fast for the terrain, but there was nothing I could do about it. The heifer was running so fast and had built up so much momentum that if I'd dallied, she might have pulled my little mare over on her nose.

We flew down the hill and headed straight for the lake. I decided to ride it out, thinking that when we got to the bottom of the hill, I would turn the heifer south and drive her around the edge of the lake. I knew she wouldn't go into the water because . . . well, cattle just didn't behave that way. Give a cow a choice between going into a lake and going around it and she'll always choose to go around it. Cattle just don't go jumping into lakes.

The heifer ran straight into the water and kept going.

COW POKES   By Ace Reid

**"Ole hoss, I jist don't know who's the biggest fool.
Her fer jumpin' or us fer holding onto her."**

Courtesy of Ace Reid Enterprises, Kerrville, Texas

I couldn't believe it, and I wasn't about to ride my mare out into that boggy, mud-bottom lake. I dallied fast and got Calypso shut down. When we came to a stop, her front hooves were sinking into the mud on the edge of the lake and I was dallied on the bitter end of my rope. The heifer was standing in water up to her chin and trying to pull us in. I had never been in a deal like this before. If Calypso gave ground, even a foot, we would be in the water and mud. I had heard stories about cowboys who had gotten themselves drowned in ponds just like this one, and I was opposed to that.

I had the option of throwing away my rope at any time, and if things had gotten out of hand, that's what I would have done. But a cowboy hates to have his rope taken away from him. It's humiliating, and you also have the problem of getting it back, since it's not very professional to leave a cow dragging a catch rope around the neighbor's pasture. We had reached a stalemate. The heifer had all four feet buried in the mud and Calypso couldn't pull her out, and Calypso had dug her hooves into the bank so that the heifer couldn't pull us into the lake. Since I was dallied on the knot at the end of my rope, I couldn't get enough slack to maneuver for better position. All I could do was wait and hope that the heifer would wear down before Calypso did.

At last she began to weaken and I got enough slack in the rope so that I could turn Calypso around and give her a better pulling angle. I spurred her and told her to get after it. Every time she hit the end of the rope we hauled the heifer a little closer to dry land, until she was about two feet from the bank. There she choked down. While she was gasping for breath, I dived out of the saddle, waded into the water, and took the noose off her neck.

I coiled up my wet rope and rode off to the north. I stopped on a hill about fifty yards away and waited to see what she would do. Instead of walking two feet to the east, which would have put her on dry land, the hussy headed west—waded toward the middle of the lake and *started swimming.*

She swam all the way across, a distance of forty or fifty yards, and climbed out on the west side. When I saw what she had in mind, I loped around to the north end of the lake, sneaked down a draw, and roped her just as she was starting back to find her cow friends. I thought she might go back into the lake and turn this into a real cat and mouse game, but she was so shocked to see me again that she bolted and ran to the south, toward my trailer.

I fell in behind her. I had no trouble driving her this time. As we neared the trailer, I kicked Calypso into a gallop, rode around behind her, slapped the rope across her back, and pointed her toward the trailer. I didn't have to drag her or wrestle with her this time. She ran straight to the trailer gate and jumped inside, just like a trained dog.

I suppose that, having failed to drown me, she had decided there was just no hope of escape.

15
Saving Cattle with the Rope

In the summer of 1980, Tom and Lawrence Ellzey and I were sorting a herd of cows that were on a patch of feed east of Wolf Creek. We found a cow that wasn't doing any good. She was old and thin, and she needed to go to the sale.

While we were looking the cattle over, we noticed that the clouds were building in the southwest. It had been a hot day and the clouds had made up rather quickly into a big blue wall that appeared to be moving in our direction. We were two or three miles from headquarters and we figured we'd better drive the old cow home before the storm hit. Lawrence had been riding Popeye, a big rough-riding moose of a horse, and he loaded "Pops" into the stock trailer and headed back to the corrals. Tom and I would drive the cow down the road and meet him at headquarters.

We got her out on the county road and drove her down the ditch. The wind had shifted and we could smell moisture, and off to the southwest we could see heavy rain falling on the Parnell Brothers' Ranch. We tried to hurry the old cow, but she was weak and wouldn't be hurried. She moved at her own pace. We began to suspect we were going to get wet. And, naturally, we had left our slickers in the saddle shed.

We'd gone about a mile and were pushing the cow as hard as we could. I was right behind her, riding through some tall weeds, when all at once the cow *disappeared*. Calypso stopped and I couldn't get her to move another step. I leaned forward in the saddle and looked down. The cow had stumbled into a hole, maybe five feet deep, that had been washed out by a culvert going under the road at that point. And if Calypso hadn't been watching her business, we would have gone in right on top of the cow. Well, that was a fine mess. The cow was wedged into the hole and too weak to struggle out of it. And that line of blue clouds was getting closer, swallowing everything behind it in a solid sheet of rain. If we didn't move along, we were going to get drenched.

Tom came over and we made medicine. He was riding Happy, a stout good-pulling horse, but Calypso was only fair on a hard pull. We pitched two ropes over the cow's horns, got our horses into position, and hit our ropes at the same time. Those nylon ropes stretched like rubber bands. The cow floundered and grunted, but she didn't pop out. The stretch in the ropes pulled our horses backward, so we hit it again. She still didn't come out of the hole, and we knew that was our last chance, because we could hear the rain storm roaring down the Wolf Creek valley.

Suddenly we were hit by a wind that must have been blowing fifty or sixty miles an hour. (Later, we saw huge limbs that had been torn off the cottonwoods up the creek.) Cold rain and pellets of hail hit our backs like buckshot, and the rain was so heavy that we had trouble breathing. In seconds we were soaked. Water ran down my spine, into my pants, into my boots; it dripped off my glasses, the end of my nose, and the brim of my hat. We pitched our ropes away and our horses staggered out of the ditch.

Lawrence had met the storm and had come back to pick us up. We dismounted and tried to open the trailer gate so we could load the horses, but the wind was blowing so hard that it took both of us to pry it open—and then to keep it from wrapping around the left side of the trailer. We threw the horses into the trailer and dived into

COWPOKES By Ace Reid

© ACE REID
9/6/87

"Now I pulled you outta the bog, saved yore life and to show yore appreciation you knock me down and nearly kill me!"

Courtesy of Ace Reid Enterprises, Kerrville, Texas.

the pickup. This was in June. Half an hour before, we had been sweating in the sun. Now Lawrence had the heater going full blast, since the temperature had dropped about thirty degrees in just a matter of minutes. We were shivering and shedding water like drowned rats. The wind blew so hard it rocked the pickup back and forth, and looking out the window we could see nothing but sheets and buckets of rain. Then, just as suddenly as it had hit, it passed and moved on down the creek.

We looked out the window and saw that we had a new crisis. The ditches were running like rivers, and the culvert was pouring water into the hole on the other side. The cow had almost disappeared, and if we didn't get her out pretty quickly, she was going to drown right in front of us.

Someone suggested that we go get a tractor, but no, that wouldn't work. She would be dead before we got back. Then we remembered that we had old Popeye in the trailer. That big son of a gun wasn't fit to ride, but he could pull a house down. We'd never found anything he couldn't pull, so Tom and I jumped out. He climbed on Happy and I climbed on Popeye. Lawrence handed us our ropes. We dallied, backed off, put the spurs to those two big horses, and plunged forward through the weeds and water. My nylon stretched and stretched and stretched, and Popeye kept going. I halfway expected that my honda would break and my rope would come back and slap me cross-eyed. But those old horses got down and the ropes held and our cinches didn't bust and our saddlehorns didn't pull out, and we jerked that cow out of the hole just as the water level reached her chin.

The next winter I saved a steer's life with my rope. It was a bitter day in February. I had put out some alfalfa hay for a bunch of scrubby, half-sick steers in the home pasture. I came up several short on my count, so I saddled a horse and went looking for the missing steers. I found all but one and drove them to the feed ground. I had to ride another twenty minutes before I found the last one, a gaunt, sorry red-neck steer that had spent half the winter in the sick pen and had managed to cheat the ranch out of a big medicine bill, not to mention any chance of a profit. I knew the scrub. He and I had looked at each other many a frigid morning in the sick pen. I didn't like him, and for two cents I would have knocked him in the head and dragged him off to the bone yard.

I found him off by himself in some timber along Northup Creek. Unlike most creeks in the Panhandle, which are wide and shallow, with gentle sloping banks, Northup had steep banks, ten or twelve feet high, and was quite deep. And at this time of year, it was covered with ice. I got behind the red-neck and pointed him toward the feed ground. He ran along the edge of the creek until he came to an old elm tree that had blown down and fallen into the water. It blocked his path, and any animal with half a brain would have gone around it.

But this scrub, who was too dumb to go to the feed ground and eat the hay I had put out, was also too dumb to walk around the tree. He plowed into the middle of it, lost his footing, and rolled off the steep bank onto the ice on Northup Creek. He wallowed to his feet and started skating around. I was disgusted. What could I do about this turn of events? The banks were so steep and the ice so slick that the steer couldn't possibly climb out. And because that big elm tree was blocking my path, I couldn't get my horse close enough to stick a loop on him.

While I muttered to myself and tried to come up with a solution, the ice cracked and the steer fell through. He slipped deeper and deeper into the water, and it suddenly occurred to me that if I didn't so something fast, he was going to drown. It would have served him right and it wouldn't have broken my heart, but cowboys aren't hired to let cattle drown. I bailed off my horse and climbed down the bank, holding onto the elm tree to keep myself from going in with the steer. I got there just in time to grab an ear as his head was going under. I pulled and tugged, but there was no hope that I could pull him out. Not only was he trapped in the ice, but he had managed to get himself tangled up in the tree limbs.

I had my catch rope and dropped the loop around his neck and threw a half-hitch over his nose. I crawled up the bank and tied the other end of the rope to the tree. That would hold his head out of the water until I could come up with something better.

I galloped back to the corral, figuring I had maybe fifteen minutes before the steer froze to death. Tom was in the corral, working with a colt. He saw me coming and knew something was wrong, since I never galloped a horse back to the corral without good reason. Thirty yards away, I started yelling. "We've got a steer caught in the ice! Get the chain saw, extra ropes, and the pickup, and meet me over on Northup!" Tom dropped what he was doing and ran for the four-wheel drive. Five minutes later, he met me over on Northup. He had loaded up log chains, the saw, and every spare rope he could find in the saddle shed.

The steer was in the water up to his ears, but still alive.

I started tying catch ropes together until I had a line that reached all the way from the steer to the hitch ball on the back of the pickup, a distance of eighty to ninety feet. While I did this, Tom cranked up the saw and started cutting a path through the elm tree. He had to cut the steer out of the tree, since the top branches were frozen in the ice. Tom shut off the saw, leaped into the pickup, and threw the transfer case into low range four-wheel drive. I waved him forward and he took the slack out of three nylon ropes. They must have stretched a good ten feet before they pulled tight.

Nothing happened. Then the ice cracked and the steer broke free. Tom sledded him out of the water, up the bank, and fifty feet beyond, just to be sure the little dummy didn't turn around and dive back in. Anyone who has ever handled steers knows that sort of behavior isn't as unlikely as it sounds. We saved the wretch, and he didn't even catch pneumonia. He was a lucky steer, and he owed his life to my catch rope—the long arm of the cowboy.

16

Uncommon
Roping Problems

Every cowboy who has ever swung a rope out in the pasture has gotten himself into situations that weren't covered in the textbook. All at once he finds himself in new territory, facing something that never happened to him before, and he has to come up with some answers, usually on short notice. All he has to work with is the rope in his hands and that double handful of stuff between his ears. Sometimes he reaches down and pulls out an ace. Sometimes he draws the Old Maid. Either way, he adds to his education and comes away with some good yarns.

In 1979 I was working for an outfit on the Beaver River. My old friend Jake Parker was foreman of the Three Cross Ranch close by, and we swapped out work. One day in June we gathered up 125 first-calf heifers. Jake wanted to brand their calves and move the bunch up into the sandhills to a summer pasture. We didn't finish the branding work until mid-afternoon, and by the time we started pushing the cattle off the meadow and up into those big hills, the day had turned off hot and humid. We knew right off it was going to be a hard drive. The cattle were sluggish and the fresh-worked calves wanted to lie down. With four men, we were short-handed because two of the boys were riding jugheads. We had to whip and shout to drive the cattle through the sandhills. The heat bothered all of us.

By five o'clock things were looking grim. The long shadows told us we had only two more hours of daylight. Our main concern was that the baby calves were trying to lie down and sneak off. If they got separated from the herd, when night came they would be coyote bait. We kept the main herd plodding along, but we couldn't hold the calves. Three of them went through a fence and ran off into a 3000-acre pasture.

Jake left his position at the front of the herd, came back to the drag, and gave me a job I didn't want. Since I had the best horse on the drive, he told me to go after those calves. I knew about roping baby calves. Any time I got to feeling like a hot-shot roper, a baby calf could bring me back to my senses real quick. God designed a baby calf so that he could slip out of his mother's birth canal, but that same design made him almost unropable. He had no horns to catch, no shoulders for the loop to hang on. Roping baby calves was almost as futile as trying to rope barn cats or jackrabbits.

I pulled my hat down and headed across the sagebrush hills, while the whistles and shouts of the other boys faded into the distance. Looking out, I saw nothing. The three calves had stopped and laid down. I thought I'd never find them. But I rode to a windmill and stumbled onto one of them. He was hot and tired, his tongue about a foot long. I slipped up to him and flipped out a perfect hoolihan— perfect except that the calf wasn't there any more.

The chase was on, up and down soft sandy hills, over sagebrush and soapweed. I threw everything at that calf but my pocket watch and small change. I threw big loops and little loops, loops over the shoulder and loops that came in from the side. He jumped through every one of them, like a dog through a hoop. At last I slopped one on, dragged him to the windmill, and tied him down.

During the chase, I had scared up a second calf lying in the brush, and I went after him. This time I concentrated on jerking slack

Matador Range, Texas, 1908. Three cowpunchers approaching an "outlaw" steer in the Croton brakes. An old animal that has lived alone for some time can be vicious and requires "stretching" before it is safe. *Ervin E. Smith photo, 1908. Courtesy of The Erwin E. Smith Collection of the Library of Congress on deposit at the Amon Carter Museum. Museum Number LC 56-88.* (Author's note: This illustrates an uncommon roping problem—a steer so big and mean he required the services of three cowboys, three horses, and three ropes.)

fast, and almost wrecked my horse when the slack I grabbed was the bridle rein. But I got him caught and tied. Darkness was falling and the third calf was nowhere to be found. I gave up and loped north to rejoin the herd, but when I stopped at the pasture gate and was about to climb down I noticed something.

The missing calf was huddled behind a sagebrush, right below my horse. I dropped the loop over his neck just as he sprang to his feet, and I managed to cheat the coyotes out of their supper. We settled the herd in their new pasture and in the day's last light, went back with a trailer and gathered up all the strays I had tied down.

Another roping problem I encountered required more cunning and less luck. Tom Ellzey and I were checking a bunch of steers on a heavily wooded pasture along Northup Creek. As we rode through the timber, we heard a steer bleating in the distance. The chinaberries were so thick that we couldn't ride a horse through them, so I got down, tied my horse, and walked toward the sound.

I found a four-weight steer off by himself. He was as gaunt as a snake and blind with pinkeye. I made a dive at him, but he heard me coming and went crashing through the brush. I drove him toward Tom, who was waiting in a clearing, then I got ahorseback. The steer was wary, as blind cattle tend to be, and we had to stalk him carefully, so that he wouldn't hit the brush again. We eased him up a hill toward a cane field, where we could get a shot at him in the open. We had our ropes loaded and ready.

At the gate into the field, the steer missed the opening and ran into the fence. I knew it was now or never, and I pitched out a Hail Mary loop. It fell around his neck, but also spooked him through the fence. That left him on one side of the fence and me on the other, with four strands of barbed wire crackling in between. My horse didn't like barbed wire in any shape or fashion, and decided it was rodeo time. He boogered and snorted and bucked, and since I didn't want to get involved with that barbed wire, I slacked my dally and pitched my rope away. Off went the blind steer, dragging my rope across the field. Tom fell in behind him and tried to pitch a second loop on him. This wasn't easy, since Tom's horse was running sideways and pointing like a big sorrel bird dog at my hissing rope.

This was the kind of five-minute job that could turn into half a day of frustration. We had to think of some way of getting a handle on that blind steer before he started running through fences. I spurred my horse into a gallop and made a wide circle around to the front of him. At about twenty-five yards away, I jumped off my horse. Tom saw what I was doing and eased off, so as not to booger the steer out of his straight course. I stood still and didn't make a sound. The steer didn't see or hear me, so he ran right past. I snatched up the rope and handed it to Tom as he rode by. The maneuver couldn't have worked any slicker if we had known what we were doing.

Another day, in that same cane field, Tom stuck his rope on a big old crossbred steer. He caught him deep, with the loop behind one front leg, and when the steer hit the end of the rope, Tom discovered too late that he had forgotten to take the slack out of his cinch. The saddle began to turn. Tom tried to shift his weight into the left stirrup to keep the saddle upright, but that didn't work. The saddle kept slipping. Tom was no quitter; he'd made a nice toss to catch that steer and he wasn't going to let go of his rope. He stayed in the saddle and rode her all the way down, until his head was dragging the ground.

At that point he slacked his dallies and yelled, "You better come get this rope!" I pitched my rope away and charged forward. Reaching down and leaning out of the saddle, I was barely able to take the rope from him. I dallied, got the steer under control, and looked back to see if Tom was all right. He had finally quit his horse and was spitting dirt. I had to hold the steer while he walked through the tall cane to find his hat and glasses and my rope.

In September of 1980 Tom got himself into another of those situations that wasn't covered in the textbook. It was one of the most hair-raising wrecks I've ever witnessed. We had spent all morning and most of the afternoon gathering 160 big steers on grass and sorting them up into bunches. While we were doing this, we found several steers with pinkeye and we cut them into a wire lot. When we had finished the sorting, we started team roping the steers in the wire lot and doctoring their eyes. They ranged in size from about 500 pounds up to 700. They were big sappy steers that had spent the

COW POKES By Ace Reid

"Old hoss, this could mean
the end of our trail."

Courtesy of Ace Reid Enterprises,
Kerrville, Texas.

COW POKES By Ace Reid

"Ole hoss, I think we jist got to the end
of our rope!"

summer on good grass. Since we would soon be showing them to a buyer, we wanted to clean them up.

Tom was riding Happy. Old Hap was a good honest horse most of the time, but he had his quirks. Sometimes when he got hot and tired he would sull, and no amount of spurring could get his attention. Well, that afternoon he must have thought it was quitting time. Tom had just roped a big black baldy steer by the neck. The steer made a dash around the pen and Tom took his dally. Then two bad things happened at once. The first was that Tom got the tip end of his glove caught in the dally. He couldn't pull the glove off, he couldn't move his hand to slack the dally, he couldn't do anything. And at the same time, Happy decided to sull.

Tom spurred hard, trying to get some slack in the rope so that he could work the dally loose, but Hap locked down, pulling the rope tighter than ever. Then the steer changed directions. Tom wasn't able to control his slack, and Happy, with his mind back at the feed trough, stepped over the rope with his front feet. When the steer hit the end of the line, pulling it tight under Happy's chest, the wreck was on. I was standing by with a heel loop and didn't know that Tom's hand was pinned. I watched and wondered what he was doing. Suddenly I realized he was in trouble.

"Drop your rope!" I yelled. Happy snorted, bogged his head, and started bucking. "Bail out, Tom!"

If Tom had told me that he was in trouble, I might have jumped down and cut his rope, but he was so intent on getting out of his problem that he hadn't said a word. Roping wrecks tend to get serious in a hurry. Later, when you go back and try to explain what happened, you can never quite figure out how the rope got where it was. Within seconds, Happy had the rope under his belly and his back heels were caught in a half-hitch, and the rope was pressing against Tom's right arm, pinning him in the saddle. He couldn't move. Hap was bucking as hard as he could with double-hocks on his back legs, and the steer circled the pen, winding horse and rider up in a deadly web. Happy bucked over to the hogwire fence, and somehow managed to break one of Tom's spur straps in the process. The steer

For almost a century, authors have been writing about "the last cowboy" and "the vanishing breed," yet the cowboy refuses to die. Next time you pass a herd of cattle on the highway, look to the rear of the herd. There, you'll see several "last" cowboys, and chances are they'll be playing with their ropes. *Courtesy of photographer, Kris Erickson.*

jerked Happy's back legs out from under him and he fell sideways into the fence.

Tom was still penned. He went into the hogwire and got a new crease in his hat, but the force of the fall also pulled his right hand free. He scrambled out of the saddle and jerked his rope off the saddlehorn. Happy staggered to his feet, unscratched but somewhat wiser. Tom walked around for a few minutes, until his hands and knees quit shaking, and then we went back to work. Happy didn't sull again that day.

It wasn't skill that got us out of that storm, just dumb luck. But like most cowboys, we figured that luck would beat brains any day of the week.

Bibliography

Books

Berlitz, Charles. *Atlantis: The Eighth Continent*. New York: G. P. Putnam's Sons, 1984.

I have an idea that the average person dates civilization as we know it back to 4,000 or 5,000 B.C., and assumes that before the time of the Egyptians, mankind had done very little worth talking about. Mr. Berlitz takes a different view. Based on his study of archaeology and ancient writings, he argues that most of the civilized advancements we have attributed to the Egyptians, Hebrews, Greeks, and Mesopotamians originated on the continent of Atlantis, which achieved a very high degree of civilization before a global catastrophe plunged it into the sea some 12,000 years ago. This book is listed here because Mr. Berlitz quotes Plato as saying that the Atlanteans were using ropes to capture bulls.

Brown, J. P. S. *The Outfit*. New York: The Dial Press, 1971.

The subtitle of this novel is *A Cowboy's Primer*. It is that, all right. I never see Joe Brown's name mentioned in lists of authorities on the cowboy trade, perhaps because he has confined himself to writing fiction, but he knows as much about modern cowboying as any man writing today. When I read this book, I was awed not only by how much Joe Brown knew about cowboying, but also by the beauty of his language. Out of the cactus and rocks of Nevada, he has squeezed milk and honey. It is difficult to write fiction about the working cowboy, but Brown has done it about as well as anyone.

Brummett, Curt. *Roping Can Be Hazardous to Your Health*. Little Rock: August House Publishers, 1991.

_____. *A Snake in the Bathtub and Other Stories*. Little Rock: August House Publishers, 1991.

There are two good reasons for reading anything written by Curt Brummett. First, he's one of the funniest storytellers alive today, anywhere. And second, he probably knows more about the craft of roping than any writer to come along since Fay Ward and Will Rogers. There isn't much you can do with a rope that Brummett hasn't tried at least once—and that goes for the bad as well as the good. Not only has he made money in all three timed events (calf roping, team roping, and steer jerking), but he has an old man's knowledge of herd loops and horse loops—and the guy was only forty-one years old when he showed them to me. Brummett should have written *this* book on the development of pasture roping. He didn't, because he was too busy roping someone else's wild cattle in those big sandhill pastures in Eastern New Mexico, but I have made abundant use of his knowledge. If he ever overcomes his addiction to roping long enough to write a book about it, it will be a crackerjack.

Coleman, Max. *From Mustanger to Lawyer.* Privately printed by Max Coleman, 1952.

Mr. Coleman, an attorney in Lubbock, Texas, printed up 500 copies of this book, with an introduction by the venerable Professor W. C. Holden of Texas Tech. It covers Mr. Coleman's sixty years in West Texas, and it's a good piece of work. It ought to be picked up and reprinted by a university press. I know about the book only because it was in my grandfather Buck Curry's Texana collection, which I inherited on the death of my grandmother in 1975. Otherwise, I've never run across it or seen reference to it.

Dary, David. *Cowboy Culture: A Saga of Five Centuries.* New York: Alfred Knopf, 1981.

This book, which won the Western Writers of America Spur Award for nonfiction in 1982, brings together in one place a vast amount of information about the cowboy, his equipment, and his techniques. If you could afford to buy only one book on the subject, this might be the one you'd want to get.

Dean, Frank. *Will Rogers Rope Tricks.* Colorado Springs: Western Horseman, 1969.

Every roper should read this book just to find out some of the things that can be done with a piece of rope. What Will Rogers (and also author Frank Dean) could do with a rope is staggering, almost beyond belief. If you think you're a pretty hot roper, reading this book will probably ruin your day, but you should do it anyway.

Dobie, J. Frank, *The Longhorns.* New York: Bramhall House, 1941.

This was one of Dobie's most popular books, and though it is regarded as a pioneering work on the Longhorn breed and the traildriving period, I have always been surprised that it contained so little information on roping techniques. But roping was not one of Mr. Dobie's vices, and he just wasn't very interested in the subject.

_____. *A Vaquero of the Brush Country.* Boston: Little, Brown and Company, 1929.
Dobie, who was not allowed to rope on his father's ranch in South Texas and never learned to use the twine himself, tells the life story of John Young, who did know how to use the twine. This is the most "cowboy" of all of Dobie's books, and it contains some excellent material on early-day roping.

Emmett, Chris. *Shanghai Pierce: A Fair Likeness.* Norman: University of Oklahoma Press, 1953.
Shanghai Pierce was one of the original cattle barons in South Texas, the kind of man who invented new styles of roping as he went along—and didn't have the time to write them down or pass them along to someone who could have written them down. Emmett's biography unfortunately tells us too little about Shanghai's use of the rope.

Erickson, John R., *Cowboy Country.* Perryton, Texas: Maverick Books, 1986.
This book describes my cowboy experiences on the old Barby Ranch along the Beaver River in the Oklahoma Panhandle. It describes the rope-and-drag method of branding we used and tells about several good ropers I worked with, including Jake Parker, Glenn Green, and Stanley Barby.

_____. *The Devil in Texas and Other Cowboy Tales.* Perryton, Texas: Maverick Books, 1982.
This collection of humorous cowboy stories contains several that will appeal to roping enthusiasts: "My New Grass Rope," "The Devil in Texas", and "Roping Fools" in particular.

_____. *The Modern Cowboy.* Lincoln: University of Nebraska Press, 1981.
In 1978 I set out to write this book describing the work and equipment of cowboys in my period and part of the country. My chapter on ropes and roping is an expanded version of the "Pasture Roping over the Years" series I did for The Cattleman.

_____. *Panhandle Cowboy.* Lincoln: University of Nebraska Press, 1980.
This collection of cowboy stories doesn't have much about roping, because during the years I worked on the Crown Ranch I didn't know much about it. But the chapter called "A Bitter Lesson" is a good

roping yarn that will bring smiles to anyone who has gotten into a wreck and wished that he'd left his rope at the house.

_____. *Through Time and the Valley.* Perryton, Texas: Maverick Books, 1983. This book, originally brought out by Shoal Creek Publishers in 1978, tells about a 140-mile horseback trip I made with photographer Bill Ellzey down the Canadian River valley in 1972. It includes the story about Sena Walstad roping a bear, and also has a chapter on Dave Wilson, one of the best ropers in the area.

Fredriksson, Kristine, *American Rodeo: From Buffalo Bill to Big Business.* College Station: Texas A&M Press, 1985. The history of rodeo, from its beginnings to the present.

Graham, Joe S. *El Rancho in South Texas: Continuity and Change from 1750.* Denton: University of North Texas Press, forthcoming.

Green, Ben K. *A Thousand Miles of Mustangin'.* Flagstaff, Arizona: Northland Press, 1972. This classic of old-time storytelling contains several passages where "Doc" Green talks about his roping, including his "damn a coward" blast of dally ropers. But like so many of the memoirs of the old cowboys, it is short on specific details. Some critics of his work would say that, not only was he not a "Doc" in the conventional sense (he had no veterinary degree), but he might not have done all the things he claimed to have done. Those of us who love his books can only forgive him and say that the world needs good storytellers more than it needs good ropers.

_____. *Wild Cow Tales.* New York: Alfred Knopf, 1979. Another Ben Green classic with some good roping stories, including a mention of his use of the Blocker loop and the fact that he carried two ropes. It is also interesting, in light of his blast at dally ropers, mentioned above, that in *Wild Cow Tales* he tells us not once but twice that he used the dally on wild stock (pp. 50 and 58). On pages 122-26 Green gives a nice discourse on various types of ropes, from rawhide to nylon.

Gregg, Josiah. *Commerce of the Prairies.* Norman: University of Oklahoma Press, 1954. Gregg, an early explorer of the praire states, gives several accounts of vaquero roping in the days before the Anglo cowboys arrived.

Haley, J. Evetts. *Charles Goodnight: Cowman and Plainsman.* Boston: Houghton Mifflin Company, 1936.
Still one of the all-time classics of the West. It was Mr. Haley's good fortune to write on such an excellent subject, and Mr. Goodnight's good fortune to find such an excellent biographer in J. Evetts Haley. I wouldn't say that this book contains a wealth of material on roping, but it covers just about everything else of interest to students of the West.

Hedgpeth, Don. *The Texas Breed: A Cowboy Anthology.* Flagstaff, Arizona: Northland Press, 1978.
This is an anthology of writings by and about cowboys. Mr. Hedgpeth, who balances his booklearning with a ranch background in South Texas, has good taste.

Hughes, Stella, *Hashknife Cowboy: Recollections of Mack Hughes.* Tucson: University of Arizona Press, 1984.
This book won a Spur award and was judged the best nonfiction book of 1984 by the Western Writers of America. It was a good choice. Mack Hughes spent his life ahorseback in Arizona and his wife Stella was with him all the time. They've got good stories to tell, and they paid the price for them.

Lomax, Alan and John A. *Cowboy Songs.* New York: The Macmillan Company, 1944.
This is the Lomax brothers' classic collection of cowboy songs. I was surprised at how few references to roping there were in them. The old-time cowboys seemed more inclined to sing about bad horses, stampedes, and love, than about their ropes.

McDermott, John Francis, ed. *Tixier's Travels on the Osage Prairies.* Norman: University of Oklahoma Press, 1940.
Contains material about the American Indian's use of the rope.

McDowell, Bart. *The American Cowboy In Life and Legend.* Washington, D. C.: National Geographic Society, 1972.
A good general survey of cowboy life through the years, with a collection of pictures that are as good as you would expect from a National Geographic publication.

McWhorter, Frankie, and John R. Erickson. *Cowboy Fiddler.* Lubbock: Texas Tech Press, 1992.

Frankie McWhorter is probably best known as a great fiddle player and as a former member of Bob Wills's Texas Playboys. But he is also one of the most knowledgeable cowboys I've ever met. He started his career on the 500-section JA Ranch in 1948, and has spent his life in the saddle, when he wasn't playing his fiddle at dances. I edited this book, which means that I tried to keep myself in the background and let Frankie tell his own stories in his own words. His stories are wonderful, and they contain some excellent material on the kind of old-time, big-ranch roping that is hard to find these days. Frankie learned his craft by roping wild cattle off wild horses, in wild country, and as far as I know, he's never given slack or thrown a dally over his saddlehorn.

Nelson, Barney. *The Last Campfire: The Life Story of Ted Gray, a West Texas Rancher.* College Station: Texas A&M Press, 1984.
This is a good memoir of an old-time cowboy and rancher. It's good for two reasons. First, Ted Gray knew what he was talking about and told it well. And second, Barney Nelson, whose husband cowboyed on the 06 Ranch in West Texas, knew enough about the subject to ask the right questions and record the kind of details that add flesh and blood to the bare bones of a story. It's no surprise, then, that the book contains several good accounts of roping in West Texas.

Norman, James. *Charro: Mexican Horseman.* New York: G. P. Putnam's Sons, 1969.
In contrast to most books which touch on the subject of roping, this one gives an excellent description of the equipment and techniques used by Mexican ropers.

Patterson, Paul. *Pecos Tales II.* Privately printed by Paul Patterson in 1984.
A nice collection of cowboy tales by one of Texas's renowned storytellers, who as a young man worked on big ranches in West Texas. Collectors of Texana will be interested in the cartoon illustration that appears on page 3, done by a fellow who grew up on a ranch near Patterson's hometown of Crane: Elmer Kelton. Elmer has won just about every honor in existence for his novels, but I believe this is his first appearance as a book illustrator.

Porter, Willard H. *Roping and Riding: Fast Horses and Short Ropes.* San Diego: A. S. Barnes and Co., 1975.
Porter has been around a long time and knows his business. This book has a lot of good material about the early days of arena roping.

Rojas, Arnold. *Vaqueros and Buckaroos.* Privately published by Mr. Rojas, Bakersfield, California. Second edition, 1981.

This book is a sequel to Mr. Rojas's earlier book, *These Were The Vaqueros.* I have failed to lay my hands on the first book, but I have high praise for the sequel. Mr. Rojas is a very well educated man whose third grade education makes one wonder about the need to keep children in school for twelve grades. He also writes well and probably knows more about the vaquero tradition than any man who ever put a pencil to a piece of paper. He knows it because he lived it and has made it his life's study. Mr. Rojas often slips into a shrill tone that makes the reader think that he is either angry or arrogant, and perhaps both. It arises from his view that too much attention has been given to the cowboy tradition in histories of the West, while too little space has been devoted to the vaquero west of the Rockies. He writes as though this were a conspiracy of "gringos," to use his term, against the Hispanic tradition. A much simpler explanation, and one that comes closer to the truth, is that while the California vaqueros were out roping bears, Texas cowboys were writing books. Mr. Rojas has done his part to correct that situation, not in his fuming about gringos but by writing an excellent book.

Rollins, Philip Ashton. *The Cowboy.* Albuquerque: The University of New Mexico Press, 1979.

This is one of the classic books on the old-time cowboy, particularly the cowboy of the northern plains. Unlike many writers of the time, Rollins did go to some trouble to gather material on the northern cowboy's use of the rope, but he writes in such a tortured, pedantic style that it is hard to translate his descriptions into common English. It is interesting that all his references to roping in the index appear under the name "lariat," and there is no listing for "rope" or "roping," even though on page 138 Rollins says that "rope was the usual term." It would fit my impression of Rollins that he found "rope" too simple a word and chose the more pedantic "lariat," in disregard of the common usage.

Russell, Charles M. *Paintings of the Old American West.* New York: Crown Publishers Inc., 1978.

A collection of paintings by the Old Master, with commentary by Louis Chapin. Included in this collection are several paintings that show scenes of Montana cowboys using their ropes.

_____. *Trails Plowed Under.* New York: Doubleday and Co., 1978.
Russell was known to his contemporaries as a great storyteller, and this is a collection of some of his stories from the Montana he knew as a young cowboy. But his stories deal more with broncs, Indians, and wild animals than with roping, which seems odd since roping was a major theme in his paintings.

Siringo, Charles L. *A Texas Cow Boy.* Alexandria, Virginia: Time-Life Books, 1980.
This re-issued version of a standard work in western literature has several good tales about Siringo roping "things that ort not to be roped."

Smith, Erwin E. *Life on the Texas Range.* Text by J. Evetts Haley. Austin: University of Texas Press, 1973.
This is Smith's great collection of range photographs which capture the Texas cowboy at work in the first decade of the twentieth century.

Steiner, Stan. *Dark and Dashing Horseman.* Harper and Row, 1981.
Steiner's book takes roping back to ancient Persia, and it is the only source I have come across that does this. It is most unfortunate that the author didn't include a list of references. If his thesis is correct— that ropes were used as tools of warfare thousands of years ago—then he has come across information that is of tremendous value to anyone interested in the history of roping. But without references, one doesn't know where to go to find the author's original sources—which should be copied and placed in libraries that specialize in western material.

Wallace, Ernest, and E. Adamson Hoebel. *The Comanches.* Norman: University of Oklahoma Press, 1969.
Contains a small amount of material on the Comanches' use of the rope for capturing wild horses.

Ward, Fay. *The Cowboy At Work.* Mamaroneck, New York: Hastings House, 1976.
A classic piece of working-cowboy scholarship, unsurpassed as far as I can tell. Dobie had a bigger audience; Ben Green was a better story-teller; Philip Ashton Rollins was better at researching and indexing; but for delivering good information in lucid English, Fay Ward stands above them all. No book I have come across contains more good solid descriptions of old-time roping methods. Those of us who write on the subject today go back to Ward's descriptions and illustrations over and over.

Whitlock, V. H. Cowboy Life on the Llano Estacado. Norman: University of Oklahoma Press, 1970.
I came upon this book by accident one day in 1993 when I was going through files of photographs in the Texas and Southwestern Cattle Raisers Association library in Fort Worth. I had never seen the book before and was attracted by its title. I turned to the index to see if it had any listings under "roping." It did—a great story about how a black cowboy named Ad roped a runaway milk wagon in Roswell, New Mexico.

Articles

Erickson, John R. "Catch Rope: The Long Arm of the Cowboy." *The Cattleman* (May 1982–April 1983): 160, 131, 131, 170, 178, 184, 178, 155, 147, 174, 200, 180.
The book you are reading began as a series of articles for *The Cattleman*, although I have added a great deal of new material that has come to my attention since I did it. I was told that the series was quite popular in the magazine, and readers seemed especially interested in my comments about the Blocker loop.

_____. "Pasture Roping Over The Years." *The Cattleman* (October, November, and December 1979): 48, 100, 110.
This series of articles, which I wrote in a barn on the John Little Ranch in Beaver County, Oklahoma, was my first attempt to combine my working knowledge of pasture roping with material I had encountered in books.

French, W. M. "Ropes and Roping." *The Cattleman* (May 1940): 16-30.
French's article is one of the oldest and most comprehensive sources on old-time roping methods I have run across. No study of pasture roping would be complete without it.

King, Chuck. "Front Footing." *Western Horseman* (January and February 1965): 42-43, 42-43.

_____. "Neck Catches." *Western Horseman* (March 1965): 118-19.
I haven't referred to these Chuck King articles in the book, because they deal with horse loops and I haven't devoted much space to that part of roping. But Mr. King is a careful scholar and these articles should be read by anyone interested in the art of roping.

_____. "The Johnny Blocker Loop." *Western Horseman* (October 1965): 52-53.

A good solid article on the elusive Blocker loop, by a fellow who knows what he's talking about. The piece also has excellent photographs and diagrams that show how the Blocker works.

Leftwich, Bill. "Conrado Gomez, Top Roper." *Western Horseman* (December 1959): 48-49.

An interesting piece on a Mexican roper who could do great things with the twine, with nice illustrations by the author. This article and the Chuck King pieces were sent to me by Dr. J. S. Palen of Cheyenne, Wyoming.

Livingston, Phil. "Trailing the Rooters." *Western Horseman* (August 1985): pp. 40-44.

Mr. Livingston writes an interesting account of an unusual and dangerous South Texas sport, hunting wild hogs on horseback.

McLaury, Buster. "Brush Cowboy." *Western Horseman* (May 1985): pp. 11-16.

When it comes to writing detailed accounts of modern pasture roping, McLaury gets straight A's. The man knows what he's talking about. He's doing today what the old-timers never got around to doing, describing in depth how they used the rope to accomplish their jobs in the pasture. In this piece, he deals with the special problems of working and roping in heavy brush.

_____. "Making A Hand in the 6666 Branding Pen." *Western Horseman* (July 1984): 52-60.

McLaury gives about as good a step-by-step description of what goes on at a rope-and-drag branding as I have run across, including a couple of paragraphs on roping technique. The story is illustrated with good action photographs by Kurt Markus.

Nelson, Barney. "The Dugan Wagon." *Western Horseman* (May 1985): 40-43.

Barney has a good eye for what's real and what ain't, and her taste runs to old fashioned cowboying, where the horse and the rope are still the most important tools. This piece tells about a group of young married couples who do contract branding and cow work in Montana, using a wagon and remuda. When she talks about roping, she speaks with authority. This story is unusual in that it gives a rare glimpse at modern women working side-by-side with their husbands. Though pioneer women often worked with the men, it isn't as common nowadays. It's an interesting piece about a bold experiment. I would like to see Barney do a follow-up piece in five years, to see what these young cowpokes are doing.

Torres, Carlos. "The Mexican Charreada: A Living Tradition." *Western Horseman* (June 1985): 90-92.
Mexican-style rodeos can still be found in parts of modern California. This account gives a summary of the differences between the charreada and its American counterpart, one of them being that team ropers can win additional points "for the complexity of the twirls of the rope prior to the catch."

Wolff, Len. "Charreada: Rodeo Mexican-style." *Texas Highways* (April 1985): 12-15.
This is a general article about the San Antonio Charro Association which sponsors rodeos sanctioned by the Mexican Federation of Charros in Mexico City. It mentions two roping events: a three-member team roping, which sounds similar to its American counterpart; and the *manangas a caballo* in which one member of a three-man team must rope a wild horse by the forelegs and take him to the ground.

ℒetters and ℐnterviews

Brummett, Curt. Interview with author. Maljamar, New Mexico. July 1989.
Dary, David. Letter to author. February 1982.
Nicholson, Dave. Interview with author. Pecos, Texas. June 1982.
Patterson, Paul. Letter to author. September 24, 1984.
Sherman, Sam. Interview with author. Seagraves, Texas. September 1993.
Streeter, Jim. Interview with author. Tandy Ranch. October 1984.
Van Cleve, Spike. Interview with author. Boulder, Colorado. June 1978.
_____. Letter to author. August 1979.

Index